Praise for Chuck Mache's
The Four Kinds of Sales People

"This book gives you powerful insights into yourself and your special qualities, as well as the personalities of other sales people."

— Brian Tracy
Author of The Psychology of Selling

"Chuck Mache has written a gem. Underneath the simple title is a powerful tool to help find your life's work. Whether you're a veteran, a novice, or even thinking about sales, this has to be on your bed-table."

— Terry Pearce
Author of Leading Out Loud

"If you're a sales person, manager, or a senior executive, you should read this book. It's an easy read on complicated people — sales people. It will remind you of yourself and those around you. In doing so, Chuck Mache will show you how to find your way to growth and development."

— Scott Cromie
Group President, ServiceMaster

"Out of dozens of sales-oriented books I've read, here is the one that finally connects the dots. What good are a bunch of techniques if you do not know who you are, what drives you, and what you can do to overcome your limitations? Read Chuck Mache's book — and break through to reach your potential!"

— Rick Sheldon
Co-founder, Intelisys Communications, Inc.

"Mache delivers his message to the center of the bull's-eye! A must-read for all in sales, and those contemplating sales as a career. It's a wonderful picture of clarity of the four sales types. Which one are you and what are you doing about it?"

—**Ross Liscum**
Broker/Owner, Prudential California Realty

"Chuck Mache's *The Four Kinds of Sales People* is a barometer for sales professionals at all levels striving for professional achievement and personal excellence."

—**Rey Hernandez**
CEO, Kemper Cost Management

"Mache is one of the most dynamic speakers I've ever encountered. Now he's written a book for sales people, sales managers, recruiters, and anybody who deals with sales people as part of their job. *The Four Kinds of Sales People* gets right to the heart of what makes people tick."

—**Jason Ehrlicher**
President and CEO, Benchmark Lending Group

"I expected another 'how-to' book on improving sales techniques. Instead, Mache's storytelling had me thinking about how this applies to my life and those that I work with. Mache addresses inherent qualities in all people—and beneficial changes to balancing your life and aligning with your true intentions. A must-read for anyone who wants to become better!"

—**Tom Hakel**
General Manager, Stag's Leap Wine Cellars

"This book is real. You won't always be comfortable, as it will challenge you to evaluate your own strengths and weaknesses as well as those on your sales team. If you're in sales, you're one of The Four Kinds and in this book you'll find yourself. It takes honesty, commitment, and discipline to uncover your 'true intentions.'"

—Dennis Harter
President, Sequoia Pacific Mortgage Company

"Ancient seekers of fame and fortune—warriors and kings—took their questions to the Oracle at Delphi, whose direction was always the same, 'Know Thyself.' Chuck Mache is a modern-day Oracle of Sales Success. If you seek improved performance, allow him to be your guide along a path of personal self-discovery."

—Dean Minuto
President, Teligent Corporation

"I've always been impressed with his speaking ability, and now I'm equally impressed with his writing. In an incredibly simple way, Chuck Mache shows you who you truly are and what you can do to overcome obstacles and be more successful...Much more successful!"

—Frans Roosen
Principle, F. Roosen Group

"A must-read for all sales reps, sales managers, and anyone thinking about selling. Finally the truth! Mache clearly paints the picture of the four types of sales people. Which one are you?"

—Billy Jensen
President, Fidelity National Home Warranty

FOUR KINDS

of

SALES PEOPLE

Your Personal Path
To Breakthrough Achievement

Published by
Elite Books
Santa Rosa, CA 95403
www.EliteBooks.biz

Library of Congress Cataloging-in-Publication Data:

Mache, Chuck, 1957–
    The four kinds of sales people : your personal path to breakthrough
achievement / by Chuck Mache. --1st ed.
        p. cm.

    ISBN 1-60070-009-8 (softcover)
    1. Sales personnel. I. Title.
    HF5439.5.M33 2006
    658.8'1--dc22

                    2006006707

Cover by Maria Ayala
Interior design by Maria Ayala
Copyedited by Melissa B. Mower
Typeset in Book Antiqua and Trajan
Printed in USA
First Edition

10 9 8 7 6 5 4 3 2 1

This book is dedicated to my family:
My incredible wife Cindy,
my wonderful daughters Shannon and Rachael,
and my terrific son Thomas.

Table of Contents

Acknowledgments

Life is full of decisions, some major and some minor. It is only after much reflection that I can determine who has made a major impact on the pivotal decisions I have made in my life. At the time, I may not have known how important the decision was, nor who was influencing that decision. Yet as I look back, I realize how important the following people were to me, and I hereby acknowledge the positive impact they have had on my life:

My wife Cindy, my lifelong partner, who is the best person I have ever met.

My Dad Steve, who taught me about a focused work ethic, and how to treat a customer.

My Mom Jeanne, who would always give me the push I needed when I sold myself short.

Jack Levar, who let me learn from one of the best sales people I have ever met.

The late Gordon Lofgren, whose funny little names for sales people would inspire me years later.

Frank McLaurin, who believed in me before anyone around him did.

Lynn Brinker, who gave me a tremendous opportunity, and taught me more about tenacity and loyalty in business than anyone I have ever met.

Dan Brinker, my close friend, with whom I grew up with in business—and continue to do so in life.

Steve Azevedo, who continues to teach me how to live life on life's terms.

Sensei Ryan Neuman, whose influence and teaching showed me the hard road to discipline.

Barney Aldridge, who gave me the means and the push I needed.

Joe Titone, always a champion of my cause.

Finally, I'd like to acknowledge everyone who is in sales, regardless of where they are on the food chain, who wants more. It is you who inspire me the most.

Chapter

1

BEFORE

As he stood and watched them enter the room, he couldn't help but reflect on his passion for sales people. Each of them was special regardless of their sales rankings within the company. He valued the fact that, on some level, each of the participants was trying to improve themselves.

Some viewed the meeting as a chance to take a break from the grind of their day to day selling. Some came looking for pearls to push their top-producing performance even higher, the best trying to get better. Some were on the way up and looking to take their selling to a level that would place them among the best. Some were top producers who, by nature of their style, were struggling with internal and external conflicts, and wanted to redirect some of their negative thinking and actions. True, they were successful, but they wanted to move to the next level and didn't know how to change. Some were there as a last-ditch effort to see if they could turn things in the right direction. And some didn't really know why they were there. They just knew that the meeting was mandatory, and they were doing what they were doing because that is what the herd was told to do. Nevertheless, he knew that on some level they all wanted to get better, do better, feel better, and leave with some tangible way to improve their selling lives. This he knew for sure, just as he knew that some wanted it more than others.

After all, at the end of the day, he was one himself: a sales person. After nearly twenty-five years in sales and marketing, from selling tires to radio advertising to mortgage loans, to sales management, to executive management, and boards of directors, he knew this much: nothing — absolutely nothing — happens in a company until somebody sells something. Until that happens, it's just a start-up that hasn't started anything. Or it's a company that is about to go out of business because it has no business. He knew this because he'd been in start-ups, small companies that he'd made large, and large companies that grew even bigger. He'd been on the streets selling and in the boardroom selling, and there was no place he'd rather be in business than right here, right now, watching sales people walk in. He was ready to prepare them.

Now he was faced with another new challenge. As the new executive vice president he was hired to get revenues on the fast track of a company that had experienced modest growth in the past two years. It was his kind of opportunity. It was another chance to be the architect of breakthrough achievement.

He had learned a lot while leading, managing, and mentoring sales executives, sales managers and sales people. First of all, if you are any good at all in sales, your life is demanding. You are a very busy individual who has to prioritize and multitask each and every day. There are not enough hours in the day and no time management course can provide you with more. You need more time. Secondly, the very best sales people did not choose to get into sales because it was easy. Only those who have failed began their journey thinking it was easy. They were mistaken. The very best don't think about easy. They think about successful selling. Easy is what

the strugglers think about. In fact, if you made a list of what it takes
to be successful in sales, it would include, among other things: cold
calling; overcoming objections; long, focused hours; dealing with
rejection; constant change; developing product expertise; gaining
trust; finding the need; withstanding threats from the competition;
working with unpredictable customers; and learning, learning, and
more learning. Now match that with what most struggling sales
people hate to do: cold calling; overcoming objections; putting in
long, focused hours; dealing with rejection and constant change;
developing product expertise; finding the need; overcoming competitive threats; learning quickly under pressure; and so on. You
get the picture. The lists are identical. The trick, he had learned, is
that the most successful sales people learn to love to do the difficult
things that most people hate to do.

As the large meeting room began to fill, he reflected on the
familiar faces in the crowd. With the exception of some of the
sales vice presidents and managers who now worked directly for
him, he did not know them by name. In fact, the majority he had
never even seen before. The familiarity came from the similarities
between the sales people in the room and those he had worked
with and managed throughout his twenty-five years.

It caused him to reflect momentarily on the journey that had
brought him to this place. Today would be about taking the company to the next level; about growth beyond anyone's current
thinking. Today was about personal growth which would in turn
lead to company growth. He knew the formula for such success
because he began using it many years ago. It was a journey that
was not without its pain and difficulties. He hoped that the people
in the room would get it a lot sooner than he had, but he knew that
breakthrough achievement required pain, or major discomfort at
the very least. He also knew that it had great reward that would
far outweigh the anguish of getting there.

He found himself recalling the time that he was a vice president in a growing company and the CEO had decided to bring in
a new Executive Vice President to take over exactly what he was

charged with doing; expanding the sales organization. He recalled the hurt that he felt being replaced, and the pain associated with knowing that the leader of the organization did not have enough confidence in him to get the job done. Although he'd kept his position as a vice president of sales, his role had been reduced and his position in the company knocked down one notch. He recalled the decision that he had to make; leave and take his talents elsewhere where he would be more appreciated, or stay, learn from this experience, and throw all of his efforts into getting better. Move on to the next opportunity, or elevate all aspects of his profession. He thought about his direct boss, the COO, walking by his office late one evening as he was busy taking his game to the next level, stepping in and saying, "I'm glad you decided to stay in the fight!" He didn't know it at the time, but his pivotal decision to attack his new assignment was the beginning of breakthrough achievement. Through the pain came the maturity, but only because he began unknowingly practicing some of the keys to personal growth. Keys such as rigorous self-examination, honesty, and the willingness to do the things that were uncomfortable, yet made him better.

He had many similar experiences and challenges throughout the twenty-five years. Some would have positive outcomes, while others would not. Many times, he would be completely in the way of himself, unknowingly blocking any opportunity to break through. It's been said that we're only ready when we're ready. This he knew too well.

He would share some of his experiences in this meeting as examples that emphasized the point he was trying to make. He knew that if he was going to be the leader of the movement to dramatically grow this company that the vast majority of the sales team would have to buy into the challenge. He knew from his experiences that they would have to personalize their own journey to breakthrough achievement. He knew that each of them would have to have a customized design for reaching new levels. He knew that they had to see and believe that there was a payoff for changing their thinking and their actions. He knew that if he were to be successful, he had to do more than just turn the "strugglers" around. He had to help the best want to get better and he had to give them the tools to do it.

"Comfort zones have no prejudices," he would say, "They dwell in many areas and on every level."

He thought about how our true intentions guide our lives, whether we know it or not. There is always an opportunity to change our intentions, but again, that requires rigorous honesty, self-examination, and the willingness to deal in the truth about our real beliefs. What we truly believe is currently guiding our actions. Our results are a product of our actions. Our actions are a result of our intentions. Our intentions are made up of our thoughts and beliefs from the conscious and subconscious mind. And, if you want to change your life, you have to change your mind.

He chuckled to himself as he looked out, observing the various sales people in the room. "Look at them all," he murmured softly, with a fondness in his voice. "They remind me of me."

He had read once that there were thirteen million sales people in the United States. Yet, as he discovered some fifteen years ago, despite all the shapes, sizes, and styles, there are only four kinds of sales people in the whole world. Not three, not six, not five, but four. He had spent the last fifteen years validating his belief as he developed sales organizations, grew companies, and created motivating environments by getting sales people to recognize which of the "Four Kinds of Sales People" they were. And in all of his years of managing, speaking, leading, mentoring, and monitoring, nobody had come up with a type that wasn't on his list. It came down to four. Recognizing oneself requires rigorous honesty. And knowing which type you are and what to do makes all the difference.

While "The Four Kinds of Sales People" wasn't an exact science (and, interestingly, that was one of the things that sales people liked about it), it was, without a doubt, an effective tool for sales people to use to assess themselves and their real agendas in their careers. It provides sales people an opportunity to pause from the daily tasks of selling to look in the mirror, get honest, determine exactly who they are, and what they are really after in their sales careers, and most importantly, how to get it. He wanted them to feel the empowerment that comes from determining which of the "Four Kinds" they were. Clarity—honest clarity—can take you places.

He was excited to share his discovery with a new group of people. His passion for helping people was his purpose and his destiny. He knew that there were over two hundred people expected to attend today's meeting. As he watched them enter the room, he was fascinated as always by the way each of the people carried themselves. While their demeanor was only part of the picture, it was one of the keys to which of the "Four Kinds" they were.

Sitting toward the front of the room was a gentleman who appeared to be organized, really organized, and prepared for the next two hours. His laptop was in front of him and powered up, a clean yellow pad with two number two pencils to the side of the pad. He was neatly attired in business casual clothes and appeared to carry himself with confidence. The man looked like he had focus. Looks couldn't tell the whole story, but he seemed like an even-tempered, analytical individual with a fairly controlled ego.

The leader watched the man as he interacted with two others in the room. From this distance, he couldn't be certain, but it appeared that the man was giving them some sales advice. The three of them were definitely engaged in sales talk and the man was giving his opinion to the two attentive listeners. In any event, personality was just one of the indicators that guided people in their determination of which of the "Four Kinds" that they were.

To the rear of the room sat a woman who apparently had brought nothing with her to the meeting but her cell phone. She was greeting people as they walked by, regardless of whether she knew them or not. When she did see someone she knew, she bellowed their name, got up and gave them a hug. She appeared to be a happy person. He wondered how happy she really was. He wondered how much dirt she got on her uniform when she played the game of sales. He wondered if she was stuck in a comfort zone or really after it. Strong and smart work ethics were factors in determining which kind of sales person she was. It certainly was not the only factor, but he wondered what she actually did with her days. Was she generating meaningful sales volume, or not?

He looked to the right of the room about halfway back and saw a gentleman doing his best to blend in. With what looked like a forced smile, he nodded his head to everyone and anyone who would come in eye contact. As he watched the man, who never spoke to anyone, it was as if he could feel him questioning his own presence there. He envisioned the man as full of self-doubt: "Why am I here? How did I get into this job? I hope things really turn around for me. Hopefully it will get easier."

Granted, these were all just first impressions and observations from a distance, and first impressions can be wrong. But the leader had spent the last twenty-five years in the souls of sales people, and he had no doubt that fear resonated from that gentleman.

The auditorium was nearly full and he was about to go through his brief pre-meeting ritual. As the side doors were closing and people began to anticipate the start of the meeting, the crowd buzz began to die down. He looked to his left and saw a man push through the closing door as he spoke on his cell phone. His words, coincidentally timed with the quieting of the crowd, carried much farther than he'd anticipated.

"Thank you," he said to the person closing the door, and then resumed his call while he walked briskly. Lowering his voice just a notch, but purposely keeping the volume loud enough for the crowd to hear, he said, "I have to go. I'm late for my meeting. People are staring at me. I'll call you at the break and we'll figure out how to save it. Don't worry, they aren't going anywhere."

Most in the crowd seemed to know him and they gave a chuckle. He was slapping hands as he made his way to a seat that had been saved for him. He was obviously an extroverted individual who appeared to be emotional, passionate, and probably packed a pretty big ego. First impression? He seemed like a natural-born sales person.

Differing personalities were just one of the criteria that the leader used to determine which of the "Four Kinds" that sales people were. The picture would get clearer when people examined their work ethic. He had learned that this alone didn't tell the whole story either. It was very possible to work exceptionally hard in sales and get poor results. Oftentimes, sales people in this position would put in endless hours but had a flaw in their selling process and, therefore, would continue to underperform. They were stuck in their inability or unwillingness to change. These were the hard cases. Getting sales people to examine their actions, actually what they do each day, begins to complete their profile as one of the "Four Kinds of Sales People." It is possible to stay extremely busy doing absolutely unimportant tasks that will never close a sale.

That is why actual sales results are so important. There is no hiding from the numbers. Based simply upon the numbers, a sales person is either:

- A top producer who ranks among the best;
- An up-and-coming top producer who is new—or newly aware;
- An individual stuck in a comfort zone refusing to go beyond his current level of productivity;
- An individual who is lost and doesn't belong in sales.

He had shorthand names for each of them, names that brought them alive and would help the audience to understand which they were.

For now, he thought about the question he was asked so often. "What if you are a good solid producer who isn't actually a top producer but does get consistent results month after month? After all, isn't the world full of those?"

He reflected on the answer he'd given time and again. "Yes, the world is full of sales people like that, and they are one reason I'm standing in front of you. If you are one of those kinds of sales people, you are in a comfort zone and you've refused to make any changes. Take the challenge and step out of that zone."

But now it was time to start the meeting. He pulled a laminated card from his back pocket; it was a card he carried for just this moment. He read it quietly to himself.

- I intend to help sales people understand exactly who they are.
- I intend to help sales people determine exactly what they want.
- I intend to help sales people find their personal path to breakthrough achievement.
- My overall intention is to inspire people to make a positive change in their lives.

He slipped his list of intentions back in his pocket and walked up to the podium.

As the crowd settled down, he poured himself a glass of water from the pitcher on the podium and looked out over the group. He used this moment to picture each of the four kinds of sales people, as he always did before kickoff meetings.

Today, as always, he followed his instincts and thought of the people he'd seen as they came in. He caught a glimpse of each one as he scanned the crowd: there was the highly organized gentleman, with his laptop open and ready; the friendly woman with the cell phone, but maybe no drive; the man working hard to blend in, and wondering why he's there. And then, there was the man who'd just entered, on the verge of late, performing in the center of his own universe. A Performer. That's where he'd start today.

Chapter 2

PARKER THE PERFORMER

The sales manager had her team assembled in the main conference room and was about to start their monthly meeting. It's the only time they meet as a group and the pre-meeting bantering was usually upbeat. Of course, the conversation was dominated by exaggerated selling stories and led by the same characters who chose a career in sales over stand-up comedy. When you spend your days doing all the things that lead to eventual sales there's something therapeutic about engaging with your peers in pre-meeting hyperbole.

The sales manager was proud of her team of twelve, and morale was running especially high on this day. She eagerly looked forward to the meeting in which she'd share the good news that once again they are the top performing team in the company. It's difficult to keep secrets from the good sales people. They have a need to know, and therefore, they find out. So in reality, everyone already knew they'd just had another banner month. However, when it comes from the mouth of the boss, there is something official about it.

True to form, only eleven of the twelve sales executives were present. The meeting was to start at ten o'clock and still no Parker. This was not an unusual occurrence. But in about three to five minutes, Parker was sure to walk through the door, apologize for being late and explain how he had been tied up closing or saving the "Big One."

Like clockwork, at three minutes past the hour, in walked Parker. "Sorry I'm late. I got tied up on the phone with a guy I've been working on for the past ninety days. I've been all over this deal. I got past the committee. Meeting after meeting, lunches, presentations, e-mails, conference calls, you name it. They're going to be a huge client and they just agreed to do the deal. This, people…is a GREAT DAY!" With that, Parker sat down and was ready to start the monthly meeting.

As one of the top sales reps in the company for the past two years, Parker was showing no signs of slowing down. It was completely true to form for Parker to enter meetings in a manner such as he just did. Not only were the sales manager and the team used to this type of behavior, they also knew that Parker's little drama scene was probably accurate. He had just scored once again. It was his job to score.

The new sales people looked on in awe and felt a slight surge of adrenalin as Parker announced his victory. The veterans had come to expect it. Some were put off by his boasting, while others were happy for his success. The rest were bewildered as to how he continued to enthusiastically achieve new sales milestones. In any case, Parker was one of the best and since he knew it, he'd be happy to explain it to you.

The sales manager said, "Parker…great job. You continue to kill the numbers. Now let's get the meeting started."

Parker felt great about himself, and with that proud, magnified grin, he briefly announced to the team, "Thank you and let me take this opportunity to say that you, oh knowledgeable one, remain a magnificent sales manager."

The sales manager knew how to handle her top producer and she wasn't going to ding him for being a few minutes late. Even though Parker's ego was larger than the company logo on the front of the building, and he could be a little irritating, he remained the top producer on the team.

Parker isn't your average sales rep. He is a Performer. He breaks company records consistently, dramatically, and with great enthusiasm. Selling comes naturally to Parker the Performer. His ability to relate to people and control a conversation, without coming across as too aggressive, is just part of his natural skill set. He's one of the best, most productive kinds of sales people. Parker and his kind are typically found among those who are at, near, or on their way to being the top producers of their company. Performers like Parker are chameleons: they rapidly adapt to the environment and styles of their customers. It follows that when prospecting they have a keen sense of determining if they have a real customer or not. And once they do, they treat that customer better than their own family members. They're the kind of elite sales person that has a razor sharp ability to determine if their products and services are a match to the potential customer's needs. In addition, they can make that determination faster than any other kind of sales person.

What's the down side? Performers like Parker can sometimes ruffle feathers. Whether through their single-minded enthusiasm, their love of the limelight, or their goal-directed behavior, relationships around performers can sometimes be strained, in the workplace and at home.

Today, like all days, Parker had difficulty sitting through the meeting. His mind was a continuous to-do list as he reviewed in his head the things that he had to accomplish to continue his sales growth. Making little notes on his yellow pad, this man had very clear intentions: to sell more than anyone and be financially rewarded for it, no matter what the cost. The only time that he really tuned in to this particular meeting was when the sales manager gave him accolades for his past month's accomplishments. When it came to selling, lack of confidence had never been a problem for Parker the Performer. With his intentions clear, he would do whatever it took to finish each month as one of the top producers. If it was a grind, so be it. That was part of the game.

Today's meeting lasted about an hour. At the end of the meeting, one of the new sales reps jockeyed his way to be near Parker as they left the room. The new rep had immersed himself in the business from the beginning and was having some success of his own. But his learning curve had not caught up to his desire to achieve, and he needed some help. He was just stuck, like good new reps get. He had already sought help from his sales manager and didn't want to admit to her that he was still stuck. "Why not go to the best," he thought to himself, as he followed Parker out of the meeting. While he knew Parker could provide the guidance he was looking for, getting him to focus his attention on anything other than his own needs would be difficult. Parker wasn't exactly a giver when it came to helping others—unless of course, it served him to do so. That was clear to even the new guy. But still, the kid thought he'd just throw it out there. "Parker," he said, "You had another great month. Nice job. Do you have a minute?"

With little sincerity, the Performer shot back, "Thanks kid. I'm in a hurry. What've you got?"

"Well, I'm stuck on a couple of my deals and I can't get the customer to move. I was wondering if…"

Parker the Performer interrupted the kid in midsentence. "Listen kid, I'm in a big hurry. This is what you have to do. The key to sales is 'finding the pain.' All you got to do is find the pain. Make their pain go away. When I do that, I make a sale. Call me Doctor Parker. Look, I gotta run. See your manager. That's what she's there for. Good luck." With that Parker was out of the conference room and off to his world of successful selling.

The kid took the hit because he was tough and made his way back to his cubicle. He thought about it for a second and decided he was too new to actually say what he was thinking of Parker the Performer.

With the kid out of his mind as fast as he had entered it, Parker made his way to a nice office that overlooked a large sprawling man-made pond that flowed along the outside of the office complex. The company was on the top floor of a three-story building that was one of many buildings. Parker's office was among a row of the nicest offices. He had earned his place on this row as one of the company's top producers. Parker went into his office, sat down at his desk, and began doing what he does best. His office was a sales sanctuary. He had awards dating from last month and well into the past. Awards that he had earned in his old company lined up as trophies do. Photographs of himself and his peers from various incentive trips from tropical places masked the walls. File rack after file rack held current clients, hot, warm, and cold prospects. Over in one corner of his office was a whole pile of "stuff." It looked like clutter. Call it the forgotten corner, where old phone messages and a pile of unread weekly and monthly reports lived. You could tell Parker wasn't big on reports — except for the ones that ranked him along with his peer group. Those he kept tacked in front of him on the wall by his desk with his name highlighted, oblivious or not caring how his colleagues might react.

One thing was evident. Parker had a system and he was very successful at what he did. He loved to sell and he especially loved the financial reward that came as a result of his efforts. His customers trusted him and all the customer satisfaction reports showed it.

Parker was concluding a phone call when his sales manager walked into his office and sat down on the leather couch. Parker's couch. In that split second, Parker remembered the one-on-one session he'd had with the president several months earlier. At that meeting, Parker had expressed his displeasure at some of the recent changes in the company's sales policies. The new couch arrived the next day. He was good at getting things he wanted.

When fellow sales people would drop by his office and make themselves comfortable, Parker could often be heard saying, "Now be careful, you're sitting on the president's couch." It wasn't long before the entire office knew where Parker had gotten the new piece of furniture.

"Parker, I want to talk about a subject that is very sensitive to you," the sales manager said. She used the direct approach with Parker.

"What's the deal? Are we selling the company?" Parker was also a fisherman.

"No, Parker. It's about your office. As you know, one of the company's initiatives this year includes an aggressive expansion plan. We're adding four new sales teams that will bring our sales organization to nearly two hundred strong."

There were twelve teams in the company, each with twelve sales reps. Even though Parker's team was number one again, top of the current teams, that didn't do anything to dismiss his concerns. Parker didn't like the thought of any changes that could get in the way of his individual objectives. Expansion in the past had meant operational wrinkles that needed ironing out. Adding four teams was no small expansion. But Parker knew that arguing about the overall strategy and its effect on the existing business would be a fruitless discussion, so he opted to get right to his point. "Just tell me the part about my office. I'm buried here trying to make us both some money." Parker was now fully attentive. His office meant a tremendous amount to him. It was his temple where he displayed all of his past accomplishments, and although his ego couldn't fit inside his office, the rest of his mind and body were quite comfortable.

"We're reorganizing the two sales floors and we're going to move you down the hall. Before you react, let me just tell you that it's a nicer office with an even better view." The sales manager, having earned her degree in Parker the Performer, knew exactly what was coming.

"Boy, I'm taken back by all of this. Here I am, the top on our team, and in the top five in the company the last three months. Number three, year to date. Now I'm hearing that I am the one who has to move." Parker was visibly upset as he poked his thumb in his chest. While Parker will go to great lengths to explain that change is not a problem with him, every time something changes that affects his world, regardless of the size of the change, Parker has an issue. He can be a very high maintenance individual. While the sales manager reaps the reward of his production, she earns every penny.

"Did you hear me when I told you it was a nicer office with a better view? By the way, it's exactly sixteen paces from this one."

"You walked it off?"

"I walked it off." The sales manager was continuing her firm approach. She'd been through it too many times.

Parker was now in full Performer mode. "That's not the point. I'm busting my ass for this company and moving my office is a big hassle for me. Why aren't any of the other people on this row moving?" Now Parker was getting heated.

The sales manager took a deep breath and faced into the storm. "First of all, I appreciate your work ethic, and it appears to be financially paying off for you. Secondly, several members of the team on 'Producer Row' are moving. Nobody has a problem with it. Just be a team player and don't sweat the little stuff. You'll have a nice office. Look at it as an upgrade."

"I've always been a team player and will remain one." Now Parker had to preach. "I just want you to know that I'm not very happy about this and it would be nice if I had a little more respect from management. I hold company sales records, you know, although I do expect them to be broken." And after a dramatic pause and another patented thumb to the chest, "By me!"

"Does that hurt?" the sales manager said, trying to make light of the situation. "Parker, it's about a fifty-foot move. It's an upgrade. You are appreciated. Let's move on. The facilities team will be by to work out the move details. I'd appreciate your full cooperation. Now we both have a lot to do. Thanks for understanding." The sales manager was out in a heartbeat. She knew he would get over it.

Parker sat at his desk. He knew that this move was not a major change, yet he still was having difficulty with that last conversation. On one hand, he felt put out that he had to move. Didn't they realize who he was? Didn't they realize that he was often recruited by the competition? He had been on such a high from this morning's sale and the accolades that he received at the meeting. During the meeting, he sat thinking to himself, "I'm Parker the Best, Parker the King, Parker the Dragon Slayer, Parker the Sniper." And now this! Suddenly, he was Parker Packing Boxes, Parker the Displaced, or simply Parker the Annoyed.

Since Parker is a Performer, his strengths can be his weaknesses. He runs so high on emotion that he can also run low on emotion. While his day started out so strong, he just let a little change get in the way of his selling day. How was he going to handle it?

ĕ ĕ ĕ

Like Parker, all Performers have the following characteristics:
- They are emotional
- They are intuitive
- They are passionate
- They are very competitive
- They are extroverts
- They are impatient
- They have large egos
- They are natural-born sales people
- They are top producers

ĕ ĕ ĕ

Parker went about his business, but now he felt that uncomfortable feeling that he experienced so often. It wasn't exactly anger. It wasn't exactly depression. It wasn't the annoyance at having to move offices. That would all work out. The feeling was one that he gets when things don't go well. It was an uncomfortable feeling. It made the day a little more of a struggle and occupied his mind far more than he would admit.

High-level sales productivity inherently brings its share of daily problems. The very best sales people view these as hurdles and not monumental challenges. It's the nature of selling. Sales people are almost always reliant upon other departments within a company to fully execute a transaction. Whether it's service, distribution, operations, shipping, administration, you name it, there is always a department or two involved in making it happen. That means human interaction and that means from time to time, there will be errors.

Parker was checking his e-mail when he received a phone call from the distribution manager about one of his orders. Apparently the order did not ship as scheduled and the customer would not receive it per the order instructions. Since it was month end, this glitch would affect Parker's end-of-month numbers. It was company policy not to use overnight shipment unless it was an absolute emergency. This would take the approval of his sales manager.

Parker didn't receive the news of the error well. He shouted at the distribution manager: "You guys are incredible. I bust my butt to make a sale and you guys can't even ship it. I swear you should change the name of your department to the 'Sales Prevention Team.' I want that order in overnight so my client receives it when I promised it to him."

The distribution manager was used to Parker's bullying and while he personally didn't care for Parker's self-centered ways, he recognized his passion and successful track record. "Parker, you know that takes approval of your sales manager and has to be deemed an emergency. And by the way, the 'Sales Prevention

Team' has a ninety-five percent customer satisfaction rating. Please accept my personal apology for the mix-up. We'll try to do better in the future." The distribution manager's comments were dry and to the point with a bit of sarcasm. He was all business.

Parker hung the phone up and called his boss. He was entering his full court press mode. "I don't appreciate the way I was just talked to by distribution. Shipping screwed up an order and I want it in overnight so that we don't lose the deal. Not only do I have to put up with their incompetence, I have to take their crap. It shouldn't be that way and I want it fixed. And you know what, I tried…"

The sales manager listened to a solid three minutes of Parker's one-sided venting. When he was through, she got the vitals she needed to approve the overnight and said to him. "Parker, it's done. I'll approve it and the customer will receive it tomorrow. They're a great customer and we don't want to jeopardize our relationship with them. And, your month is still intact. Buddy, we're all on the same team. Relax."

"Thank you," Parker said and he hung up the phone still stewing, at only a slightly lower temperature.

The sales manager cleaned up Parker's relationship issues with distribution as best as she could and approved the overnight. Meanwhile, Parker went about his day.

ẽ ẽ ẽ

Performers are driven people with a character defect of impatience. They can be very reactionary which sometimes translates to a pompous, self-centered, and unreasonable demeanor. The very best Performers have this flaw harnessed and have learned from their experiences. They've come to realize that without a "team" effort, they would be far less successful. Therefore, the best of them consciously cultivate the habit of practicing within their own company the same relationship and problem solving methods they use while selling. After all, a Performer will never unleash negative behavior on prospects and customers. The best ones are positive within the company as well. Parker had a lot to learn.

❧ ❧ ❧

Later that day while driving home, Parker continued to have that uncomfortable feeling. Maybe it was of missing something in his life. He couldn't pinpoint it. He knew that sales were a grind; in fact, life was a grind. He had never known any other way. To be successful, Parker the Performer felt that he had to step on internal toes when he needed to. You had to be tough to survive and nobody was tougher than Parker the Performer. Still, he was bothered by his feeling and maybe even by the need to step on toes.

Sales can be very lucrative and Parker was living that dream. He owned a beautiful home in a new development, wore the finest clothes, and drove a beautiful Corvette that he was sure was the envy of all on the road. "Victory Red" was the color and it had four hundred horses in that V-8. While it was loaded with everything, Parker really got a kick out of the push button starting capability on the end of his key chain and the throaty growl of the engine. He drove the complete package that really impressed people—at least it seemed so from Parker's viewpoint.

He sat at a red light and thought about how his day had started out so good as he closed a deal that he'd been working on. So what if he was late to the meeting, the best sales people are kings. He would have liked to help the new kid who asked for advice but that's the sales manager's job and time is money. He was still irked about having to move offices and the whole conversation he'd had with his manager about the move. He thought about how he had gotten the overnight approval on the shipping error.

"Operations need to get their act together." Parker wasn't big on empathy for others. He reflected on the "grind" of the day and said quietly to himself, "Nobody ever said it would be easy." With that, he maneuvered his prized possession into the gas station to fill up.

❧ ❧ ❧

Performers are passionate people whose emotions can be either their friend or their enemy. The better the Performer, the better they have a handle on this issue. It follows their productivity and the more they "harness the beast," take control of their negative side, the better their chances of staying in the selling zone. You won't find long-term top producers whose emotions are out of control during a major percentage of their selling day. Performers are challenged by this every day, however, and the best recognize the danger of running too high or too low on emotion. Parker the Performer knows this, but it doesn't make it any easier for him to stay focused and positive consistently.

Parker grew up in the area and he has been getting gas at Steve's Service Station since he was a kid riding with his parents. Oddly, it has had the same owner all of these years. Steve was an old man now, although he looked ten years younger than his eighty years. His service station was in mint condition. It had changed over the years, as he'd weathered all of the conversions from conventional full service stations with few pumps that included auto repair work, all the way to the forty-eight pumps on eight stalls, a car wash and mini-mart that stood today. Parker flashed back on the Steve who'd towered above him in earlier years. Then, Steve had stood over six feet tall with a build that included very muscular arms and shoulders. They weren't the "show muscle" that was built in a gym like the physique Parker had sculpted as an adult. This was work muscle constructed from twisting wrenches, mounting tires, and whatever Steve's previous life had brought him.

For as long as Parker had been going to the station, it was a thriving place. Steve's work ethic was a big part of that. Location didn't hurt either. In earlier years it was a fairly rural area and Steve made his name with the three-stall garage where he kept some of the finest auto mechanics busy six days a week. Steve built his business on honesty and hard work and he treated his customers like they were part of his extended family.

Parker was always perplexed as to why Steve hadn't retired many years earlier; he was certain that Steve could financially do so. In any event, Parker pulled into the stall, got out, swiped his credit card, and began filling up. Steve was repainting his white curbs and looked up to give Parker a wave. Parker walked over to say hello to Steve as he'd done for the past fifteen years whenever he had the time.

The years had been good to Steve but eighty is eighty. Today when Steve stood he was a little crooked, age had taken much of his muscle, given his hands a little tremor, and he looked over his bifocals as he greeted Parker. Same embroidered name on his shirt, same pocket protector, same tire gauge in his pocket, and the same warm smile.

"How's that Corvette runnin'?" That seemed to be Steve's first question every time.

"It's going fifty-five while it's getting gas, Steve." Parker was quick witted and it always made Steve laugh.

"Well," Steve said, "Are you making lots of sales down at that big outfit of yours?"

"Yeah, I'm doing great, Steve. Sales have never been better."

Over the years Steve knew this much about Parker. He was either sky-high or down in the dumps. Despite the words, today Parker looked like he was having a downer. Steve never probed into people's business and didn't offer advice unless he was asked. There wasn't any kind of person that Steve hadn't dealt with over the years. Kind, caring, forgiving, angry, jealous, fearful, you name the personality and the emotion, and Steve had experience in dealing with them. That's what forty-plus years in this business will bring you.

Parker and Steve made small talk about the weather, family, and baseball. As they spoke, you could hear horns honking as people either drove by or left the station. Steve would smile and wave at each driver. Parker was always amazed at the volume of exchanges that would go on in a short period of time.

Parker had to say something. "Steve, you're amazing! In about two minutes, eight people have honked and waved at you. It's always like that every time I talk to you. What's up with that?"

"You salesmen always exaggerate," Steve kidded. "But since you asked, I'll tell you this much. I've seen a lot in my years here on this corner. I've met all kinds of people with all kinds of dispositions. Lucky for me, everyone needs gas for their vehicles. I've made lots of friends who owned stations like mine. Most of them are dead or nearly dead now." Steve chuckled without a smile. "I learned early on that the happiest people don't focus on happiness. They focus on helping other people. No matter what business they're in."

Just then, Steve saw a lady struggling to put oil in her car. "Parker, I gotta run. Say hi to your mom and dad when you talk to them," and with that, Steve was moving across the lot to the lady in need. Parker couldn't believe how fast Steve could move for his age.

He liked Steve and his station was always clean, but Parker certainly didn't think Steve was an expert on success. It was an old man in a gas station. Happiness is winning the quarterly contest and that trip to Hawaii. Parker's intentions were clear.

❦ ❦ ❦

Weeks clicked off and Parker continued his assault on the company quota. His sales were thirty percent over the previous year and his income followed. The thing about Performers is that while they are not the most detail-oriented people in the world, they execute the life of a sale very well. They begin with the end in mind and are full of confidence. They are very visual people and have a built-in capability that allows them to project in their minds a positive outcome to their selling efforts. In other words, once they've determined that they have a "real" prospect, they convince themselves that the prospect will become another customer. From this point on, Performers' actions follow their beliefs. Clear intentions.

This thinking earned Parker his quarterly contest as he finished in the top ten during the quarter. The company's monthly sales meeting was held on a Friday and management dressed in Hawaiian shirts in recognition of the contest and its winners. A five-day paid vacation in Hawaii was a great perk, but more importantly to Parker, it was the recognition of being a winner. As the vice president of sales called up each of the winners, they were given a lei by the president to wear as a trophy. As the lei was placed around Parker's neck, he yelled to the crowd, "The thrill of the kill!" Everyone laughed, including the president. Parker was pumped as he lined up with his peers and a member of the marketing department took their picture for the next company newsletter.

Later that afternoon, when the less committed were starting their weekend early, Parker was making follow-up calls on the leads he had developed during the week. He knew people were generally in a good mood on Fridays and securing appointments for the following week would be less difficult than on Monday. As Parker concluded a call, one of his fellow sales people came in. Parker knew that this guy prided himself on receiving information before it was announced. While he wasn't quite a conspiracy theorist, he did have his share of paranoia. In any case, he loved to focus on stirring things up more than he did on sales, and he did his best to take people with him on the mental journey to the land of overreaction. The guy did, however, have a good hit rate on early information.

"Parker, have you heard the latest?" the Chirper said as if he were about to announce the most earth-shattering news that had ever hit the company.

"No, but I'm certain you're gonna tell me." Parker was half paying attention.

"Keep this between the two of us, but they're taking away our individual admin. assistants!" The Chirper should be so enthusiastic on his sales calls.

"How do you know this?" Parker was now at full attention.

His livelihood was being threatened.

"I know this," said the Chirper.

"How do you know this?"

"I know this."

"How?"

"I know!"

"Okay, okay. Stop!" Parker leaned in. "When?"

"Monday!" the Chirper was in heaven. Giving early news to Parker was such a thrill.

Parker grilled the Chirper for everything else he could think of but that was all he knew. "That would be one of the dumbest moves they could make," Parker said over his shoulder to the Chirper as he strolled down toward the coffee maker.

The moment Parker knew he was out of the Chirper's sight, he changed direction and marched directly to his sales manager's office. He stormed in, unannounced, and said, "This is the most ridiculous thing I have ever heard. What are you people thinking?" Parker was worked up. He was good at letting his emotions get in the way. "I just heard that you are taking away our admin. assistants. Do you realize what that will do to my revenue?" Without pausing to allow the sales manager to answer, Parker barreled on. "I'm a top producer in this company and I rely on my admin. to do all the things that allow me to stay in front of customers. My admin. assistant completely follows the job description that you guys laid out for the position. She handles all the sales support issues and keeps the non-sales crap off of my back. She's terrific. And so am I. My numbers are thirty percent over a year ago. The company is kicking butt. First you make me move offices and now you're taking away my admin? What's next, a comp cut?" By this point, Parker was in full Performer high maintenance overreaction. He was angry; in fact, he was borderline rage. He continued on for another few minutes until he had to pause for air.

"Are you done yet, Parker?" the sales manager asked with a

firm look that matched her tone. She'd been down this road too many times.

"I just think this is complete crap! What more do you guys want from me? All I do is top produce. That's all." That was his best Parker the Performer turned Parker the Persecuted. Same guy, different mood.

"Listen to me, Parker. I don't know where you heard what you heard. It's true and I'm going to ask you to keep it quiet until Monday." The sales manager let her comments marinate for a moment.

"So it IS true! You guys are amazing." Parker stood up to leave. The persecuted always create an us versus them stance.

"Sit down, Parker. I'm not finished. As usual, whoever told you this did not have the whole story. Now I'll tell you the whole story but I want your word that you will keep it between us. It affects the lives of many people. Some people will be let go on Monday, and I'd like you to think of them for a second. You and your admin. assistant are fine and staying intact." The sales manager's laser eyes were now burning through Parker.

He started to get that feeling of discomfort that he gets when he lets his emotions override his better judgment. His selfish ego was being exposed. He didn't like himself very much right now, but he was feeling some happiness over hearing what he thought he'd just heard.

The sales manager went on to explain that the top ten percent of the sales people were retaining their admin. assistants; for them, it would be business as usual. The remainder of the organization would share a pool of assistants under a new plan that had been tested and developed over the past several months. Several on the administrative staff would be reassigned and others would be terminated due to the reorganization. It was all going to happen on Monday.

Parker was humbled. He apologized for his outburst as the sales manager reminded him that they'd been down this road together on many occasions. She asked him to think about his behavior here today. She suggested that he would never treat a customer as he had just treated her–and asked him to explore within himself why he would act this way within his own company. She emphasized his tendency to a roller coaster personality that takes him to highs and lows on a frequent basis.

"You know, Parker," she said as she lowered her voice to a whisper. "People get in your way, and you just mow them down. A person keeps doing that, and they run out of supporters. Not to mention friends." Now she leaned in and stared directly into his eyes. "After a while, it doesn't feel so good."

Parker nodded his head in agreement. He gave his assurance that he would keep things confidential, apologized again for his outburst, and left his manager's office. He walked back to his office, carefully avoiding the Chirper, closed his office and left for the weekend. On the drive home he was embarrassed that he hadn't for a moment considered the outcome for the people who were about to be terminated. They would not even have jobs and all he could do was think about how it would affect his sales. He didn't like himself very much right now and wanted to shake this feeling as fast as possible. He also didn't like the way he had once again let his emotions take control of his interaction with his sales manager. Parker was not happy and he knew that something had to change for this Performer.

❦ ❦ ❦

Performers have large egos and at times it will appear that they are out of control. In fact, they sometimes are. This usually occurs within their organization, and is ignited when there is a change or mix-up that threatens their immediate sales success. It may be that miscommunication occurs in operations, accounting, customer service, shipping, you name it. It's not unusual for the cause of the mishap to be traced right back to the Performers themselves. However, this is usually determined after they've already done the damage.

❦ ❦ ❦

Parker pulled into the gas station at around five o'clock. Traffic had been horrific, even for a Friday. He recalled Steve's comments about helping other people that he had so easily discounted the last time they talked. "The key to happiness is helping other people, or something like that?" he said to himself.

Maybe there was something to it. Could the old man be on to something? There he was over in the corner of the lot. This time he was planting petunias under the sign that displayed the station's gas prices. It was an impeccable flower bed with multiple colors. Steve was busy adding purple and red to the mix.

"Hey Parker, how's she runnin'?" Steve was speaking of the Corvette that Parker had gotten washed at lunchtime.

"Just great, Steve. How are you doing? I see you're hard at it." Parker was often on a high at the end of a hard week. But despite his words, Steve could tell that Parker was in a little funk today. Steve turned back to the flowers. While tending to them, he thought to himself how life was a real struggle for Parker the Performer and how it was too bad that he didn't take more time to appreciate all that he had.

All of a sudden there was a tremendous screech that lasted for what felt to Parker like an eternity. Parker was so startled that he jumped back about two feet. Steve just looked up directly at the squealing tires as dark smoke and burnt rubber filled the air. Then there was a horrific sound of the impact of an accident. Metal on metal.

"That's a bad one! Parker, call 911 right now! Tell them there's been a bad accident and people are hurt!"

"But how do you know that?" Parker said.

"Just do it now!" Steve said more sternly than Parker had ever known him to be.

Parker looked at the wreck and then back toward Steve. But Steve was gone. As in, where did he go?

While Parker called 911 to report the accident, he looked around for Steve and out at the crash. Everything was so surreal at this point. The street was complete pandemonium. Shattered glass, pieces of cars, the smell of burnt rubber, punctured radiators hissing, and people screaming.

A man in a black Yukon had run the stoplight and hit a woman in a Volvo station wagon broadside at the driver's door. People were crowded around the Volvo trying to get inside. Parker finished the 911 call, and found himself right next to the wreckage. He had no recollection of walking from the flower bed to the middle of the street. Later he would reflect on the peculiarity of Steve's disappearance and his own appearance at the actual wreck.

At that moment, an ambulance and a fire truck pulled up. It had been less than ten minutes and Parker felt enormous relief to see the emergency crew. The firefighters brought out the Jaws of Life equipment to free the woman, who was not conscious and was bleeding from the head profusely, as head wounds do. On top of that, there were children and a baby screaming in the back seat. Four people total in the Volvo.

The firefighters were struggling to pry the door off so the paramedics could get to the woman. Crushed though it was, the solid door wouldn't budge. Using their giant tool, they maneuvered it to gain leverage but the door was too mangled. Police were now on the scene and attending to the man in the Yukon. He was unhurt and two police officers were talking to him. Another officer was directing traffic amidst the flares that had been set up on the roadway. She was doing her best to get traffic to move along.

The frame of the Volvo was so impacted that none of the doors would open. The car had actually taken on a U-shape from the collision. The firefighters were continuing to attempt to get in the car when a voice suddenly boomed, "Step aside!"

Parker was surprised at how the firefighters so willingly cooperated with Steve. They stopped what they were doing and moved over. There Steve stood holding a very heavy crowbar. He was holding it with one arm, the bar perpendicular to the ground like a staff. With the strength of a man forty years younger, Steve flipped

the crowbar up to his other hand, wielded the flat end into a corner
of the door, and drove the bar deep into the mutilated machine.
Then he let out a loud quick exhale as he popped the imbedded
crowbar with both hands and his body. With that, the door flew
off the car, allowing the professionals to take over.

Parker could not believe what he had just seen. He was still
holding his cell phone when one of the paramedics pulled his head
out of the wreckage and said, "You! Come here!"

Parker looked behind himself to see if the paramedic had been
yelling to someone else. No such luck. He was talking to Parker.
They had removed the unconscious mom from the car, strapped
her onto a gurney and put her in the ambulance. The firefighter
and the paramedics were getting the children out of the car. A little
boy appeared to be hurt, though maybe it was only cuts and bruises from the impact. The paramedics were taking special precau-
tions with the baby who would be thoroughly examined. Luckily,
the baby had been in a car seat. The child in the far rear appeared
to be completely fine. When the paramedic pulled the unhurt girl
out, Parker saw that she looked to be about eight years old. She
was screaming for her mother. The paramedic who had called for
Parker looked at him and said, "Take this girl. Talk to her while we
get her family taken care of. I'll be back for her. Tell her it's going
to be okay." The paramedic gave the little girl to Parker. How was
the paramedic to know this was Parker the Performer, who spends
most of his time thinking about himself?

Struggling to push away thoughts of panic, Parker looked
around for Steve. There he was, back at the gas station. In fact, he
had just gotten out of Parker's car, having moved it from the gas
pump. Steve was walking over to his flower bed and did not look
at Parker, who stood holding the little girl's hand. Parker needed
Steve right now to help him with the little girl. But Steve knelt
down in his flower bed with his body turned away from the wreckage. Parker thought about yelling to Steve but it was two hundred
yards away and the commotion would drown his words out.

The little girl stood by Parker's side, holding his hand. Her body was erect as if at attention and she was sobbing. Tears rolled down her bright red face as she stood shivering and holding this strange man's hand. She was looking at her mother, who was being attended to by paramedics. Her brother and baby sister were loaded in the other ambulance that had arrived once it was determined that so many people were involved in the accident.

Parker had no idea what to do at this point. This is the last situation that he wanted to be in and one that he had never been in before. He knelt down on one knee and put himself at eye level with the little girl. Her squinting eyes now moved from her mother and were looking directly at Parker.

"Everything will be okay. Your brother and sister didn't look like they were very hurt and they're taking care of your mommy right now." Parker was giving it his best shot.

"I don't want my mommy to die! I don't want her to die! Please don't let her die!" The little girl was frightened to death as she screamed her words through her crying.

"Listen to me. That's not going to happen," as he used his best confident voice. "I promise you that she is going to be okay." With that Parker prayed in his head like he never had before. He asked that the mother make it through her injury.

The little girl leaped into Parker's arms and put a bear hug around him that nearly knocked him over. Parker could feel her trembling and now Parker's eyes welled up with tears.

"I'm scared. I don't want to lose my mommy. I love her," she said.

"It'll be okay. Trust me." How many times in his life had he said that? "Your mommy just got hit pretty hard but she'll be okay. The doctors will take care of her." Now Parker was hugging back as hard as the girl.

"Please, God, don't let my mommy die!" The little girl was praying.

Parker started silently praying with her. He said he was sorry for every time he was selfish and didn't think about others. He asked for forgiveness for not being grateful for the things that he had. He said he regretted how he had treated people who were only trying to help him. He wished he could take back a lot of his self-serving actions. He prayed for the mother to pull through this mess. Now tears were rolling down Parker's face, too.

At that point, the paramedic who had given Parker the little girl came back for her. "Come on, sweetheart. We have a special place for you to ride and then you can be with your brother and sister."

The little girl released her vice grip on Parker. Just before she left, she reached up with her tiny hands and wiped the tears from Parker's face. "Goodbye," she said, now appearing to be a little stronger.

"Thanks, man. You did good." The paramedic patted Parker on the side of the shoulder.

"No problem." Parker, who was still on one knee, was dazed. What just happened? He watched as the little girl got in the ambulance with the other kids who had both been treated for minor cuts. A thorough examination would take place at the hospital. He stood up and ran over to the paramedic and found out what hospital the family was being taken to. He planned to call later that night to find out about the mom.

The cleanup crew was busy moving the metal. Traffic cops were still attempting to get a smooth flow going and the two ambulances left for the hospital. The driver of the Yukon was being handcuffed and put in the backseat of a police car. Apparently, he failed a field sobriety test. Parker flashed onto some of the many times he had driven while under the influence.

Parker the Performer used his shirttail to wipe his eyes and face as he made his way out of the street and onto the lot of the gas station. His shirt was soaked through from sweat, his tan pants were dirty, and his shoes were filthy from the whole event. He walked over to Steve who was just finishing planting his petunias.

Steve looked up over his glasses and stood up. It took him a while. He was smiling at Parker. "You alright?" Steve said.

Parker nodded and asked, "How did you take that crowbar and…?"

Steve interrupted Parker midsentence. "Here are your keys," he said, as he reached in his pocket and handed them to Parker. "I just moved your car. I didn't take her for a spin." Steve tried to lighten Parker up.

"Thanks." Parker was talking slow and his mind was still on what had transpired. "I'm gonna go home and take a shower. I'll talk to you later, Steve." He turned and made his way to his Corvette.

He was about ten feet away when he heard Steve say, "Hey, Parker!"

Parker stopped and turned around. He was still very much dazed.

"You took fine care of that little girl for a minute and gave her hope. That was good work. I'm proud of you." Steve's demeanor turned to serious.

"How did you know that from here? You know what? Never mind that question." Parker had enough for one day. "I'll talk to you later, Steve. Thanks."

❦ ❦ ❦

Later that night Parker phoned the hospital and learned that the mother was going to make it. She had suffered a severe concussion, a broken collarbone, and required some stitches to her head but would make a full recovery. Additionally, the kids all were fine. They had the standard cuts and bruises that an impact of that nature delivers. They were all very lucky.

Parker was overjoyed with the news. He hung up the phone and let out a "YAAAAAAHHH" at the top of his lungs, as if someone had just cheated death. He lay in bed later that night and was very thankful for the day's outcome. In fact, he felt better than he'd felt in quite some time. He couldn't pinpoint his newfound feelings except that he was overjoyed by the news that the little girl still had her mother. He spent the weekend reviewing the events of Friday afternoon. The sound of the crash, Steve telling him to call 911, the crowbar incident, the paramedic, the little girl, the drunk, and the mother's positive outcome. Especially fresh in his mind was his interaction with the little girl.

"Thank God, she still has her mother!" Parker said to himself.

❦ ❦ ❦

Monday morning rolled around and Parker was back at the selling game. Today, however, Parker the Performer was different. For the first time in as long as he could remember, nothing was bothering him. Usually the weight of the tasks that were in front of him completely consumed him: target list of potential clients, presentations to prepare, follow-up sales calls, and all the detail required to successfully close deals and maintain a large customer base. Victories, headaches, and disappointments, it was all part of the selling game. But those things were not eating him like they had in the past. Granted, he was focused on them, but they were not weighing as heavily as they had just last week.

He was pouring coffee in the break room and still somewhat puzzled by his newfound attitude when the new kid who had approached him weeks ago for advice walked in. The kid did not acknowledge Parker and this time Parker understood why.

"Hey kid, about before. I was pretty busy at the time. But if you want, I can spend some time with you later today on your deals. I have about an hour at around four o'clock. You interested?"

The kid thought aliens had taken over Parker and he let it show. "Are you talking to me?"

"Yeah, I'm talking to you."

"Man, Parker, that would be great. I'll come to your office at four o'clock." Parker could see the kid's whole demeanor change; the kid was happy.

Parker went back to his office and before he attacked his morning he wrote the following e-mail to his sales manager:

"First of all, I know that your job is difficult and you're constantly being pulled in many directions. I also know that I'm not the only sales rep on your team, although sometimes I act like it. I want to apologize for the hard time I gave you about the move last week. I know you'll take care of me. Also, I could have approached the admin. layoff discussion with more empathy for others. Once again, you showed that you're doing your best to take care of me. I'm going to continue to put up great numbers and I just want you to know that I'm also going to work harder on the things that seem to cause internal conflict. I recognize my part in all of this. Thanks for everything you're doing."

He reviewed what he had written and before he hit the send button added one final sentence: "By the way, record month coming our way! YES!"

Then he hit the send button.

While Parker was a high energy person, like most Performers, today was different. He genuinely felt good about himself. His intentions had always been to sell more than anyone at any cost. Empathy for others had never been high on his list. His success came from focusing his energy on using his natural ability to sell. It's what all Performers did. But something was changing in Parker the Performer. Yes, he wanted to be the best, and during some months he was. His number three ranking in the company had him well into the six-figure income annually. On paper, he was a tremendous sales success.

Parker knew that as a Performer he was emotion driven and at times struggled with the highs and the lows of the sales environment. Being a victim of his own emotions could cause some time management difficulty. Functioning in one of his "lows" was usually caused by a negative experience during the workday. Perhaps he lost a customer. Perhaps he didn't get the customer he was expecting to close. Those were minor in comparison to his reaction when things internally didn't work out like he had expected. In any event, a negative experience could damage his short-term productivity. Too often he ran the risk of sinking into that "low." When this would occur, productivity would plummet and his day would come to a halt.

Parker had always been aware of his emotional ups and downs. Like the best of Performers, he had learned to guard against staying down too long and was experienced at dealing with the difficulties in returning to the selling state of mind. He was where he was because he had learned to battle through this emotional roller coaster. But the battle was making him tired.

Does the job have to be such a grind? Am I the cause of almost all of my issues? These were the questions he pondered as he thought about his recent interactions with the shipping department and his boss. For the first time, he thought about how they must feel when Parker the Performer's ego is going crazy. He was constantly boxing everyone into a corner with his words. This was perhaps what made the job such a "grind."

Now, for the first time, Parker was rethinking his intentions. He had a new concern about how he was treating people and his personal struggle with the emotional "roller coaster." While maintaining balance in his life had always been a challenge, Parker recognized that he was going through too many highs and lows for no reason. Parker was realizing that he could get awfully worked up over little issues. Compared to what he had just gone through with a little girl who had nearly lost her mother, his issues were nothing. On top of that, it never occurred to him to think of the other people around him and what they might be going through. His only focus had been on getting the sale, taking care of his customer, and getting more sales. He was true to his intentions.

He went through his day in much the same manner as he had in the past. He was completely focused on sales growth. However, he made one slight change. Parker the Performer was going to consider the feelings of those with whom he worked. When issues arose that in his opinion impeded his sales goal, he would take a lighter approach. He would replace his aggressiveness with assertiveness. He would keep the same focus on problem solving but with a touch less of the reactive, maniacal Parker. He would make a concerted effort to really weigh the impact of all the issues, and communicate in a less attacking manner. He would focus on having empathy for other people and to the best of his ability not let his ego and strong will get in the way. He wanted to continue to feel better about himself, as he did when he helped the little girl. He would help others whenever he could—and with no agenda other than to help. He expected nothing in return. He just wanted to continue to feel good. He would make sure that he remained focused on his mission of selling.

At four o'clock, the kid came into his office. He had a list of five questions for Parker that he wanted counsel on. The kid took a cautious demeanor as he laid his issues out. Parker could tell that the kid had the potential to be a solid producer.

Parker was entirely focused on the kid's feelings and needs. Amazing in itself, since this may have been a first for Parker. He was not just paying attention to this kid, but he was consciously focusing on someone else, someone who wasn't a potential sale, and someone who couldn't help his financial bottom line. It was all new to Parker and he did his best not to let his mind work its way back to his own to-do list. It dawned on Parker that he had spent his entire sales career using his intuitive skills to close sales and had rarely put these skills to use outside of this effort. Having spent most of his time concerned about himself, his sales, and his victories, he now felt good helping someone. It got him out of himself for a minute. These feelings were new to him. He was feeling happiness without chasing happiness.

Parker took one question after another and the kid made notes throughout the discussion. As they were talking, the sales manager walked by Parker's office. Within seconds, she reappeared outside the window with a puzzled look on her face. Parker flashed a smile; she returned the same and moved on.

"I'm half crazy!" Parker thought to himself. Then Parker spoke and gave the kid his full attention. "This is what I'm seeing and hearing. I believe you have tremendous potential in this business. It really all boils down to what your true intentions are. I thought I was clear on mine, and for the most part I am. I'm going to make a few tweaks to my intentions. Kind of a new and improved me, if you will."

The kid was all ears. He wanted what Parker had. He wanted to be a top producer. Parker continued. "This is what I would do if I were you because this is what I do. I would manage by dollar opportunity. I try to be a perfect manager of OPPORTUNITY. It looks like you've learned to qualify a prospect rapidly, which will save a tremendous amount of time. It didn't take me long to learn that either. Some people it takes forever. Some never get it."

Parker was getting animated now. "Once I've determined that I have a real opportunity to work with, I focus my time on the gatekeepers and decision makers that will turn my efforts into actual sales. Too many people have fear around this. Have no fear. Rejection is your friend. If you're not getting rejected, you're not making sales." Parker was in full Performer mode now.

"I use a very simple system. Some people subscribe to a complex time management system. I'm sure it works for them. But I'm not a real detailed analytical person. This is what I do. Which opportunity is hot? Which opportunity is warm? Which opportunity is cold? I simply focus on hot until the deal is closed or until it is determined that it should be in one of the other categories. Then I try to move warm to hot or cold as fast as possible." Parker went on, "This one is big, kid, so listen up. Do everything that you can every day to advance your deals into sales. If you're not advancing your opportunities to a potential 'yes' or even a 'no,' then you're not selling."

"Also, I sparingly work the cold pile. The reason for this is, if I have a cold file, it is truly cold. That's how good I am." A Performer's big ego is never going to go away. Parker was rolling now. "Three simple buckets categorized as hot, warm, and cold.

Nothing keeps me from working the hot and warm piles or it's a bad day. Are you with me?"

The kid looked up from his yellow pad that he was feverishly writing on and nodded his head. Parker could tell he was really taking the information in. Parker the Performer emphasized the importance of not getting bogged down by non-sales activities. "For me, if this starts occurring, everyone will hear about it. But that's me. You have to find your own style that works for you."

After an hour they wrapped up their discussion. The kid was beaming. "Thanks for your help today, Parker." He was genuine with his appreciation.

"Remember what I said. Manage by opportunity. Three piles. Focus on hot and warm piles. Advance them every day. You do that and you'll keep your focus, make great money, and win some awards. Got it?"

"I got it. Thanks again." The kid left to attack his sales opportunities.

Parker sat back in his chair and thought about what had just occurred. Just last week he didn't have time for anybody or anything that didn't help his personal cause. Had this last hour away from his personal business hurt or helped him? How important was that hour to him personally?

He looked at his screen saver that had his intentions scrolling across. It read:

"My intentions are to be the top producer on my team and in the top five in our company, qualify for every bonus and incentive program, and increase my income by thirty percent over last year. Nothing will keep me from my intentions."

He pondered the power of clear intentions. He had lived and breathed this intention and considering his status year-to-date, he was very confident that he would realize his intention. "Amazing stuff," he said to himself.

He thought again about the little girl and the accident last week. He thought about Steve's actions and behavior: his fast movement at the time of the accident, the crowbar, and the way he returned to his flower planting while Parker dealt with the little girl. He wondered what Steve's intentions were. He laughed to himself that he was even thinking about these things.

Parker then reviewed his e-mail, as was his standard practice at the end of each day. It didn't matter if he was in the office or on the road, it was the last thing he did each evening before trying to shut things off for the night.

His admin. assistant had gone home for the evening and Parker discovered that he had an issue with the billing department that had upset one of his customers. Normally, he would delegate this to his assistant, but this was one of his best customers and he wanted some resolution immediately, if possible. He had thought this problem was solved after last month's billing, but apparently not.

He made his way over to the accounting department and was disappointed to see that the place was almost empty except for the accounting manager and one of her staff members. This is where Parker usually did his Performer thing and would bring out the "Do you know who I am?" attitude that originated from his massive ego.

As he walked into the department, he felt that surge of impatience that so often overcame him. This time, however, about as fast as he was picking up his walking pace he began to slow down. He thought about what he was about to do. Did he really have to resolve this issue right now? Would eight-thirty tomorrow morning work out just as well? Couldn't he direct his admin. assistant and then follow up with the billing supervisor later? Most importantly, wasn't he about to take a "go to war" attitude to resolve the problem? While he was confident he would have resolved the issue, how would he feel afterward if he took his usual Parker the Performer approach? How would the supervisor feel?

"Why am I thinking about how anybody feels?" After some consideration and with some apprehension, he realized it wasn't necessary to revert back to old behavior over this minor issue. He didn't want that "grind" feeling to come back anyway. He decided to wait until tomorrow and kept walking by the office that the two accounting people were in. As he passed, he overheard one of them talking about his desire to purchase a new car, and that he was going to go to the dealership at lunchtime the next day to look. Parker's first thought was, "Figures, they aren't even working." Then he thought about how ridiculous his first thought was. It was after-hours anyway. "Relax," he said to himself.

He turned around and walked back into the accounting manager's office. "I'm sorry to interrupt, but I couldn't help overhearing your discussion about buying a new car."

The accounting manager knew Parker and the staff member knew of Parker. They braced themselves for a Parker-like comment or tirade. Instead, he said the following, "I happen to be friends with that dealer. If you'd like, I'll call him for you and make sure you get taken care of." The accounting manager made a rapid recovery from her shock at Parker's act of kindness and introduced the staff member to Parker.

"If you want I can call him right now for you. It will only take a minute and believe me, he loves calls like this." Parker was helping again.

The staff member was very appreciative and went on to explain that this would be his first new car and he wasn't sure if he could afford it. He had always driven used cars and his current one was on its last leg.

"Don't tell the dealer that," Parker said in a half-kidding way. He'd never taken the time to count the number of new cars he had owned in his life. The staff member excitedly told Parker the model he was interested in. Parker pulled out his cell phone, called the dealer, gave him the staff member's name, and set up a lunchtime appointment for him for the next day.

"Parker, thank you very much. This is exciting!" The staffer was overjoyed.

"Listen, if you want me to look at the deal for you real quick, I will. Get all the numbers. You should be good at that." Accounting joke from the peddler. "I'll do my best to help you get a good deal."

The accounting manager briefly wondered what had happened to the real Parker. The staffer was nearing giddiness and Parker felt uncommonly good again. The accounting manager looked at Parker. "Was there a business issue you needed help with?"

"You know, it can wait until tomorrow. Thank you though." Then he thought to himself, "What am I saying?"

"I'll be looking for something in the morning and I'll make sure it's handled on our end." The accounting manager was appreciative of Parker's act of kindness. The staff member thanked Parker again before Parker went back to his office to shut down for the night.

As Parker walked back to his office, he thought about how the whole interchange only took five minutes. He had just helped someone in only a few minutes. Again, he felt pretty good.

His screen saver on his computer was still scrolling with his intentions:

"My intentions are to be the top producer on my team and in the top five in our company, qualify for every bonus and incentive program, and increase my income by thirty percent over last year. Nothing will keep me from my intentions."

He sat down and went into his computer to alter his screen saver. Meeting these goals would earn him well into six figures. Why change the intentions? He knew, and he rewrote his intentions to include:

I intend to help people along the way.

A few more adjustments and his new screen saver read as follows:

I intend to be the top producer on my team.

I intend to be in the top five in our company.

I intend to qualify for every bonus and incentive program.

I intend to increase my income by thirty percent over last year.

I intend to help people along the way.

Nothing will keep me from my intentions.

He logged off for the evening. He would make the same changes on his laptop when he got home later that night.

❧ ❧ ❧

For the next several weeks, Parker the Performer consciously operated with his newly added intention in mind. His sales continued to climb but this time his career didn't feel like such a grind. Big egos and emotional balance are the challenges of all Performers. Parker found that if he took the time to help people along the way to achieving his goals he had better control of his ego. If he had better control of his ego, he wasn't experiencing the emotional "roller coaster" that he'd been victim to so many times in the past. When he got out of himself, he felt better about himself. When he felt better about himself, his emotions were intact. When his emotions were intact, he stayed in the selling zone longer. With these changes, life wasn't such a struggle for Parker the Performer.

❧ ❧ ❧

Another week ended and Parker was heading home. The Friday traffic didn't seem to bother him as it once had. It was time for a fill-up and Parker sat idling in his Corvette at the light across from the gas station. He had not seen Steve the last few times that he had gotten gas. In fact, he hadn't seen or spoken to Steve since the accident.

He looked across the street and was happy to see Steve at the station. This time he was sweeping up cigarette butts, little wrappers, and the other small debris that gathers on the busy property of a station of Steve's size. Steve had manufactured his own version of a dustpan with a handle on it. He had cut a one-gallon aluminum gas can so that it was opened at an angle at one end. Then he nailed it to an old broom handle so that he could hold the dustpan by the handle in one hand. In his other hand he had a broom. Without bending down, Steve could move across the lot, sweeping small pieces of garbage into the can. Parker was certain that some manufacturer made long-handled dustpans for just that purpose, which you could purchase at most hardware stores.

"That's Steve," he said to no one.

The light turned green and Parker made his way across the street and onto the lot. As usual, the place was jamming. There was a pump open and Parker pulled in. He wasn't sure if he was going to tell Steve about the changes he made or his newfound happiness.

Once he had the fuel flowing into his car, Parker started walking over to see Steve. As he got closer, he bent down and picked up a wadded empty cigarette pack. Steve noticed the small act of kindness. When he got to Steve, he made a jab step left, acted as if he was dribbling the balled up trash, bent down and slam-dunked it in Steve's dustpan. Then he popped up, extended his right arm to Steve and they shook hands. Parker thought to himself that someone should talk to Steve about his tight grip.

"You must have had a pretty good day," Steve said with a smile.

"Actually Steve, I've been having good days." Parker emphasized "days."

Steve waved to a customer and looked back at Parker. "Sales must be pretty good."

"Sales are always good, Steve. You know, I haven't seen you since that Friday we had the wreck. That was pretty hairy."

Steve noticed that Parker said "we" when he spoke of the wreck. "Damn drunk drivers!" Steve said with a firm tone. "I understand that the family's all going to be fine. One of my customers is a nurse at the hospital the paramedics took them to." He went on to tell Parker what he already knew about the mother's concussion and broken collarbone. "The kids just had some cuts and bruises. All of them were minor."

Parker jumped in with, "Yeah, I'm glad to hear that. I called the hospital that night and got the same story."

Steve was impressed that Parker would do that. He had a hunch why Parker had been having good days.

"You know Steve, I wasn't sure if I was going to tell you this, but that accident changed something in me." Parker's tone was quiet and humble.

"Is that so?" Steve asked.

"After that night, and the way I had to get involved, I took a look at my life and how lucky I really am. You know, I'm one of the best at what I do." Once a Performer always a Performer, but Parker was stating a fact.

Steve was fully focused on Parker now. He wasn't scanning his station as he usually did when they had a conversation.

Parker continued, "There's always been something missing. It felt like something was wrong. I felt that if I were going to be successful at the level I desired, I had to be extremely aggressive with people. Really, I never took the time to consider anyone but myself." Now Parker was getting choked up. "I didn't plan this." He was looking down at the ground now and Steve saw a tear fall from Parker's eyes.

"Hey, don't mess my lot up!" Steve said as Parker gave one of those choked up laughs.

Parker went on, "It really feels good to help people with the little things in life. I don't get so full of myself, and I'm still knocking the crap out of my goals. It fills a hole, Steve. I've finally realized I don't have to bully my way around to get things done in my business. I hate bullies, Steve, and I really don't like how behaving like one made me feel. Giving a little helps keep me balanced."

"Yeah, I know what you mean, Parker. If you want to go crazy, try to have everything go your way. It's just not possible." Parker listened to the old man like he never had before. "I learned a long time ago not to sweat the little things. And by the way, everything's a little thing. Things like that wreck a few weeks ago remind us of that."

Parker reflected on how he had spent his whole life doing the talking. There was much to gain from listening. The only time he really listened was when a customer was talking. But, ultimately, that was self-serving hearing.

"Anyway son, you did a nice job helping that little girl. You really helped her get through a rough moment. It looks like she helped you too." Steve was smiling at Parker.

Parker had pulled himself together now. "So have you, Steve."

Just then Steve noticed a woman at the air machine attempting to put air in one of her tires. Parker saw it too and said, "Go for it, Steve."

Parker the Performer turned to go back to his car, and Steve made his way across the lot with his broom and homemade dust-pan to help the woman. Parker was once again amazed at Steve's agility.

Steve was almost to the lady's car when he yelled back to Parker. "Remember Parker, if you want to keep it, keep giving it away!"

That was Parker's intention.

Chapter

3

PAULA THE PROFESSIONAL

The president of the company was here because it was policy that executives make field visits twice each year. It didn't matter whether they were directly involved in sales and marketing; they were instructed to meet customers and witness firsthand the sales people at work. This was done to ensure that all organizational leaders appreciated the customer and to eliminate as many barriers as possible between departments. It followed then that Operations, IT, Legal, Accounting, and even Human Resources spent two times each year in the field in hoping to further teamwork over the long haul. In fact, this customer-driven philosophy was one of the reasons Paula had chosen to work at this company two years ago.

The sales managers always made sure that executives in the field were placed with the very best sales people. They had played this game before and the last thing that they wanted was for the management team to give negative feedback to the executive vice president (their boss) about one of their own. So he planned to use a sales rep whose personality most matched the president's. Paula was an analytical and even-tempered professional. She also happened to be one of the most consistent top producers over the last six months.

The president had spent the last two days in other regions visiting with the sales reps and customers. He didn't grow up in sales and his corporate lifeline was through accounting with the standard progression from VP to CFO to executive vice president to president. He was very much a people person, extremely savvy, and was doing a solid job of leading the company. He was the right person for the job and unafraid to make tough decisions.

The sales manager was to pick up the president at the airport and drive him to their first meeting where they would be joined by Paula, and then would meet their first customer. The two met and greeted each other at the agreed upon area in the airport. After the usual small talk, the president surprised the sales manager by saying, "I'd like to cancel our field visits today and spend some time talking with Paula about her territory." The president continued, saying, "As you know, we're always looking for ways to improve our productivity in the field and I know Paula is one of the best. I think I would get more value out of seeing how she manages her territory than visiting customers today. I've been doing that my last two field visits. Okay with you?"

"Not a problem," the sales manager replied while heaving a silent sigh of relief, knowing that Paula would be up to this. "We were going to take you to our secure accounts anyway and have you shake hands with them," he joked, smiling. "I'll call Paula and have her handle canceling the meetings. I'll let her know you want to talk territory management and we can meet her in the office in about an hour."

They met with Paula in the main conference room of the regional office. Paula the Professional's career hadn't started in sales. She had a college degree in psychology with a minor in political science. Her original aspirations had been to continue her post-college education and get her teaching credential. But when she found herself burnt out on education, and with ambitions for a richer lifestyle, Paula was prompted to change her career path. This was her second sales position in the past five years as she successfully made a transition to her current job. Prior to this one, she had held an inside sales position that more closely resembled a customer service job.

Today, as planned, the office staff and the facility were in top form. The sales manager wouldn't have it any other way. Paula had never met the president, and after introductions and pleasantries, they got down to business.

The president kicked things off by saying, "Paula, you have a big territory and our data indicates that you are gaining market share in each of the last four quarters. You took over this territory when you joined our company. I'm particularly interested in how you've been so successful. What can you tell me?"

Paula the Professional was a skilled communicator who used excellent grammar as she spoke of her history. "Once I decided on sales as my career choice, I made a commitment to myself to be the very best. I am a disciplined individual and I always make certain that I do the things that are required to excel."

"What kind of things are you talking about?" asked the president. Meanwhile, the sales manager leaned back and drank his coffee, knowing that Paula had things under control.

Paula continued, "Well, the first thing I did was make sure that I associated myself with a company that had solid training programs. Having no background in sales, it was imperative that I join a company that was committed to training for new employees as well as ongoing training for its people. When I was shown our library of training CDs and actually got to sit in on a class for a few minutes prior to making my decision, I was really impressed. I knew I didn't just need product knowledge, but additional selling skills training. After all, my first sales job wasn't exactly hard core.

Of course, that's why I opted to start there." Paula went on. "The next thing I did was apply the same learning methodology that I had used in school. I was attentive in the classroom, made detailed notes, and studied my notes at home during the evening. I even made a list of questions each night before I went to bed and made sure that I addressed them with the trainer the following day."

Paula the Professional stayed on track. "One observation that I made was that while our company was very good at product knowledge training, we spent little time on actual selling skills. It reminded me of college in that they don't teach you how to study. They just feed you the information and test you on it later. While I made sure I was strong in the product knowledge department, I had to do something on my own to really improve my selling skills."

"I spent the next six months learning how to sell. By day, I'd work my territory. I anchored myself in the territory where I learned how to prospect and determine if I was working with a potential 'real' customer. Then I learned how to close that customer. Of course, I purchased every CD and read every book I could get my hands on that would improve my game. I'm a pretty determined person," she said with confidence.

At that point, the president was fully engaged and the sales manager loved it. "Get to the meat, Paula! You're holding back on the boss," he said proudly.

Paula turned her laptop around to face the president. "This is a list of every potential customer in my territory." As she pointed to a column on her spreadsheet, she said, "It shows right here if they are a current customer or not. This column shows how I rank each of my customers and prospects. The bottom line is this. From this list, you can see each company, its size, who it's buying from, what it's buying, why it's buying from them and not me, and the last time that I called on the company. It includes my personal action plan to make them our customer. Over here, you can see the accounts that I've converted to us just this year."

In the back of her mind, Paula knew she would have liked to have been better prepared. "Winging it" never made her comfortable but the president's enthusiasm assured her that she had obviously pulled off her impromptu presentation.

"Paula," he said, "your territory management is as good as I've seen." The president expressed how refreshing it was to visit with a sales person who was as organized and tactical as she was. Paula the Professional looked over at her sales manager, who gave her a nod of approval.

❦ ❦ ❦

Later that day, as Paula filled her car's tank with gas, she reflected on the meeting. As a professional, Paula's mind was on her work even outside the office, even while pumping gas. She was pleased that her sales manager had called her on the phone to tell her that the meeting had gone well. Certainly she knew that, but it was always good to hear. And since self-promotion was not her style, it felt good to know she was on the "radar screen" of the main boss.

She finished fueling and pulled her car over to the station's mini-mart to buy a bottle of water. As she was getting out of her car, she saw a familiar sight. The homeless man who usually stood on the corner on the edge of the station property was in his position. With traffic lights and active businesses that had a lot of people traffic on each of the corners, he could have chosen any of the four corners. Paula had an idea that Steve's empathy toward him had something to do with where he chose to stand.

Paula had been seeing the man for the last year and had given him a few dollars from time to time as she left the gas station. Paula had read that over 20% of the homeless population were military veterans, and of that 20%, nearly half had served in Vietnam. This man wore a gray baseball cap with the profile of an American eagle's head as a logo on the front. The cap was as filthy as the man himself and Paula always noticed how angry the eagle on the cap looked. The homeless man's salt-and-pepper hair was in a scraggly ponytail and his cap was pulled down low over his brow. He spent much of his time with his head lowered, making it difficult to see his eyes. Whenever Paula gave him money, he would look up and smile. He always said, "God bless you, missy," by way of thanks.

His eyes were set deep in his head and surrounded by skin that had been severely weathered. When he did smile, it was clear that he had no front teeth. His beard was pure gray and as long as many years of not shaving would make it. He wore an old gray sweatshirt that was as dirty as his cap. His sleeves were pulled up to his elbows and both arms had faded tattoos. Paula always assumed that he got the tattoos during his time in the military. He had on old running shoes and his oversized blue jeans had holes in the knees. The jeans were as filthy as his sweatshirt and cap.

"Our friend has it pretty rough," Steve said as he appeared next to Paula. It seemed Steve always had the knack for appearing out of nowhere; Paula found that was a little eerie.

"We sure don't have much to complain about," replied Paula, without taking her eyes off the man. Then she looked around the station at all the cars that were filling up. She looked back at Steve and said, "Business looks pretty good, Steve."

"Like you said, I don't have anything to complain about."

Paula always admired how personable Steve was to all of the customers. He must have said hello or thanked people for coming in all day long. She thought to herself how he would make a perfect Wal-Mart greeter.

"How are sales going with you?" he asked Paula.

"They're going well. I'm a little concerned about the future. I think I've picked all the low-hanging fruit in my territory. If I really want to excel, I'm going to have to target some accounts that are in pretty deep with my competition." She briefly wondered why she was explaining all of this to an old man in a gas station.

"I'm sure you'll figure it out. You know, I remember when foreign cars first came to our country. I must have started doing work on them some time in the 1970s. I had four mechanics at the time. My three-stall garage used to be over there," as he pointed to where the restrooms now stood. "I kept three mechanics busy on the inside and one on the outside. Anyway, it seems as though I had two kinds of mechanics—those who embraced the foreign cars and those who didn't. The ones who didn't were always calling the cars junk, saying that they wouldn't be around very long. Some even refused to work on them. I think they were just afraid of change or something. Of course, the ones who refused to work on them didn't work for me for very long." He gave a little smile.

"I was always kind of impressed with the mechanics who focused on figuring those cars out. They weren't afraid of taking those things on. Did you know that before it was Nissan, it was called Datsun?"

"No, Steve, I didn't know that," Paula said with a slight look of confusion on her face. She wondered where that one came from.

Steve thanked Paula for the business and she went in and bought her water, returned to her car, and began to head home to take her evening run. As she left the lot, she rolled her window down and handed the homeless man a dollar.

He was grateful as he gave her his trademark, "God bless you, missy!"

Even though he was outside and she was in her car, the air still reeked of stale alcohol, tobacco, and just plain bad smell. At that moment she recalled more of the article that she had read on homeless people. It said that over 75% of the veteran homeless has alcohol, drug, and/or mental health problems. As she drove home, she felt sorry for the man and wondered about the horrid past that had taken him to this low place.

❦ ❦ ❦

Exercising was a terrific release for Paula. She had always participated in sports while growing up. In fact, for eight years she had dedicated her time to a traveling soccer team. From age ten to eighteen she participated on a team that was always ranked nationally and that won the state cup championship on two different occasions. While soccer was a major commitment on her part as well as her parents', she wouldn't have traded it for anything. She traveled throughout the United States, made some lifelong friends, and really got to experience the challenges and rewards that go with high-level team sports.

Three things were certain about being successful as a team at that level: First, you had to have very good players; Second, and perhaps most importantly, the entire team had to be passionate about what it took to win; And third, she was very fortunate to have an excellent coach in her last three years. She knew she'd never forget the highs and lows that go with competing at that level, and although she declined several scholarship opportunities in college, she maintained a regular fitness routine.

Paula the Professional attributed much of her sales diligence to those disciplined years as an athlete. In recollection, whenever she was confused about her soccer future and considered not continuing, her performance suffered. Consequently, her playing time would be reduced. When her intentions were to excel, she would excel. Not surprisingly, her playing time would increase.

❧ ❧ ❧

Paula used her evening runs to review her intentions. She viewed this time as an opportunity to focus on the importance of being completely honest with herself about her true business purpose. Not long ago she spent considerable time researching and gaining an understanding of the value of clarifying her intentions. Her interest on this subject began when a friend of hers had given her a CD on the subject of "true intentions." She had really connected with the belief that tremendous opportunity to reach your desired goals exists when your conscious and subconscious mind are completely in sync. She had learned that this was not possible unless people were willing to be completely honest with themselves and commit to the challenge of self-examination. Too often she had witnessed people in her peer group make outrageous claims of the future success they were planning, only to fall well short of their plans. She believed it was because their "true intentions" were not fully clarified. Consciously they planned to achieve great results, but in their subconscious minds, another game was being played. "The Doubt Game" as she had learned to call it, was full of statements in the subconscious like this:

"I doubt if I'll really make it."

"I doubt if I'll really put the time in that is necessary."

"I doubt if I really deserve all of this success."

"I doubt if I'll get that lucky."

And on and on goes "The Doubt Game," full of sabotaging thoughts that keep people from reaching higher levels. Their "true intentions," therefore, were very unclear because of the conflict between the conscious and subconscious mind. The difficult thing, she had learned, was even identifying the thoughts in the subconscious that were counterproductive to the conscious thoughts.

Her newfound beliefs in the potency of "true intentions" were strengthened as she reviewed many of the outcomes in her life, from her challenges and victories in soccer to her academic progress. She was convinced that if you could truly define your intentions and make them a working part of your everyday life, they would become a reality.

Paula the Professional had clarified her sales intentions at the beginning of the year and placed copies of those intentions in visible places within her home. One copy was taped to the mirror in the bathroom off of her bedroom. Another was on the refrigerator, and still another copy was taped to the wall in her home office. They read:

I intend to be an expert in all of our products

I intend to be an expert at overcoming the key objections

I intend to be an expert at following our selling steps

I intend to be an expert at territory management

I intend to work hard and turn this knowledge into sales

I intend to earn well into six figures this year

❦ ❦ ❦

While running, Paula repeated her intentions quietly to herself and evaluated her progress with each. She was on target year to date and it looked as though she could accomplish her income goals.

Paula thought back to her first week of training in her company. She was pretty certain that many of her peers considered her too amiable and reserved to make an impact in sales. Granted, Paula understood that she didn't have the personality makeup that lends itself to the extroverted aggressiveness that she saw in some other sales people. But she knew she was focused and assertive, and the results showed. This morning's meeting with the president had confirmed that for her.

❦ ❦ ❦

Professionals like Paula share the following characteristics:

- They are even tempered
- They are analytical
- They are logical
- They are quietly competitive
- They are internally passionate
- They are patient
- They have controlled egos
- They are top producers, in line with the more visible Performers

While the best sales people are very good listeners, Paula the Professional maximizes this skill set. Although she's less outgoing when rapport building than some of her other top producing peers, she makes up for it with her tactical expertise in the sales process. Like all Professionals, she has a formalized set of qualifying questions that she weaves into her daily selling. She relies on these questions—and meticulous attention to the responses they elicit—to carefully qualify potential customers. She's excellent at asking questions that allow the potential customers to articulate their current situation. As they're doing so, Paula looks for any "pain" they are currently experiencing. Then she asks questions that steer the customer to a logical solution to eliminate their pain. More often than not, the solution can be found in one of her products.

Paula recalled a seminar that she had once attended entitled, "The best sales people in the world talk less than their customers." She had learned that the very best sales people in the world ask very good questions that allow their customers to sell themselves. The very best sales people in the world "connect" their products and services to their customers. A very orderly, systematic process matched Paula the Professional's style perfectly with her personality.

❦ ❦ ❦

She remembered parts of these seminars as she ran the five-mile course she had designed. It took her from her home, down the hill, along a frontage road and up into a city park in which there were two beautiful lakes. The five miles ended about a quarter mile from her home. So she would walk for about five minutes to cool down and hydrate from the forty-minute run. Once she got home again, she routinely spent ten minutes stretching on a mat in one of her extra rooms.

Tonight, something was bothering Paula the Professional. She'd come to know this uneasiness that she was now feeling, but she was having difficulty identifying exactly what was disturbing her. She connected this mysterious aggravation to when she began linking past outcomes in her life with her past intentions. Granted, she had successfully transitioned to a full-fledged outside sales position. Additionally, it appeared she was on track to realize her sales intentions. But tonight, like many nights of late, that uneasy feeling was back. It wasn't exactly fear, and it wasn't that she was lacking in fulfillment. She had prided herself on doing the things required to avoid failure, yet she was really struggling with this one. She knew it was in there, in her subconscious, but Paula decided to let it go for the weekend.

❦ ❦ ❦

On Monday morning, Paula was in her home office when she got a call from her boss. He sounded a bit apologetic as he started saying, "I know I took you out of the field on Friday to meet with the president, but I'd like to talk to you later today. I need your help on a team project."

Paula already had her calendar up on her computer. "I have three appointments today and I was planning on coming into the office anyway this afternoon. Will three-thirty work for you?"

Paula went about her day in the usual manner. Her three appointments were with existing customers that she was attempting to sell deeper into. As she had learned, in her business, customers would often use more than one vendor in her trade and eventually migrate to one of them as they outperformed the other. Paula's company had performed well and she had a successful day continuing her market share growth.

On her way to the office to meet with her sales manager, she drove by the offices of a large potential customer that wasn't using her at all. She recalled when she was new in the territory and she had made an appointment to meet with the owner. She had been warned that this gentleman had a negative experience with her company several years ago and that he was now fully engaged with her main competitor. Like a good sales person, that hadn't stopped her from setting up an appointment with the man. At the time, she was surprised she got the appointment with such ease.

That had been two years ago. She knew that her sales skills at the time of the appointment weren't nearly where they are today, but Paula still felt the sting of the experience she had come to call "The worst sales call of my life!"

Each time she drove by this business, her thoughts would take her in many directions. The first thought was of the dramatic growth that would occur if she could penetrate this potential account. It would increase her personal sales by 25%. It would dramatically grow her market share within the territory. It would put her in the running for the President's Club award, given annually to the sales person who brought in the largest new customer. It would turn an extraordinarily difficult individual into a customer — and it would make her feel successful each day as she drove past the building.

Aside from all those benefits, she knew that her product line was a better fit than the products that they were currently using from her company's competitor. That misfit was especially frustrating to Paula the Professional; she was certain that her products were superior to those being offered by her competition.

Her thoughts would always return to the very uncomfortable experience that she had at her one and only meeting with the owner. For that reason, she had never made another attempt at securing his business. Perhaps that is what really bothered Paula the Professional. On the other hand, playing it safe had worked well for her.

During "the worst sales call of her life," it became apparent to her that the man had made the appointment just to voice his disdain for Paula's company. Apparently the sales person before her had overpromised and completely underdelivered. On top of that, management at that time made no attempt to save the business or the relationship. In the opinion of the manager then, the man was too difficult to deal with.

Paula recalled the sting of the owner's words: "I wouldn't do business with your company if it was my only option. You guys completely screwed me and I'm not the kind of guy who ever forgets that. Now get out of my office so I can do business with your competition."

"Ouch!" she said to herself as she thought about that day.

She made her way to her regional office and left those thoughts behind as she entered. It was a campus setting located on a hillside surrounded by acres of lawn and beautiful landscaping. The three large buildings on the campus each had two floors. The exterior of the buildings were mirror-like, giving it a modern look.

The regional office was located on the first floor and Paula entered, greeted the usual people, and stopped at her office cubicle where she left her briefcase and laptop. Her office was one of five large cubicles that lined the window that looked out on the hillside. They were considered the nicest sales offices and were reserved for the best producers. Paula the Professional was one of those. The remaining sales people had smaller cubicles in a bullpen setting in the center of the office.

From a distance, the sales manager saw Paula coming and gave her a wave. She entered his office and he got up and closed the door. He reinforced how well Paula had done with the president and Paula thanked him for the compliment.

The sales manager got right to the point. "As you know, last month the company did an internal survey of the sales people regarding our company training program. The results of the survey showed that our material is outdated, or "stale" as the majority described it. It also showed that the delivery of the training was too dry, and that the troops wanted the program to have more enthusiasm and entertainment." He went on to explain that the sales people surveyed had been specific about three training objectives that they wanted:

- More product knowledge on the core products.
- The tools to overcome the top three objections.
- The training to be fun for participants.

He explained that he had thirty days to put together a program for the president's review that would deliver on those three objectives. The president had decided to keep the training department out of this project and wanted to see what actual field sales people could come up with.

The sales manager went on to explain to Paula that he had selected two of the veteran sales people to develop the program. While he was concerned that developing the program might take away from their selling efforts, these two people were top producers and certainly had the respect of the entire sales force. Additionally, they were very articulate, outgoing, fun, and confident public speakers. After an initial meeting, which laid out the goals of the program, he had delegated the project to them and agreed to meet in two weeks, which was halfway to the completion date. At that time, he would expect the first draft of a completed program.

"We met last Friday afternoon after I took the president to the airport for his flight out. That was the halfway point to our due date," he said. Much to his disappointment, everything was still in the idea form and there was no first draft.

The two sales people had come up with the concept of using hit movies as a theme to the training. The plan was to do spin-offs of movie themes and put posters around the training room and hallways with the two Performers' pictures superimposed on the actual movie poster. They had mentioned *Training Day* as the first poster. They felt it was a good way to announce the training and have some fun.

"Then," the sales manager said, "they want to give prizes away toward the end of each session if the sales people answer certain questions correctly. It will reinforce what they have learned."

"It sounds pretty good so far." Paula meant what she said.

"Here's the problem, Paula. While we have two weeks left to get this done, these guys don't have anything more than what I've told you. There's no content."

A smile came across Paula's face because she knew the two sales people the manager was talking about. They were great sales people but they always focused on their own best interests. Paula, who might have predicted the result, began to sense why she was there.

"I asked them about the guts of the training. You know, product knowledge and a program on the top three objections. All they worked on was the 'fun' part." The sales manager gave a laugh and Paula joined in. There were only two weeks to go, and that was it. He explained that he had then inquired about the content of the new training program. "I knew the answer to my question, but I had to ask anyway."

Putting on his best imitation of one of the sales people, the sales manager responded to his own question, saying, "Uh, we haven't done that yet." He went on to tell Paula that he had made a mistake when choosing the team. He had selected people who were natural sales people and while they were great at selling, they weren't going to get this done. While they could certainly present the program to the troops, they lacked the skill set to develop and design a program around the goals.

With a smile, her manager said, "I know now that I should have included you in the beginning of this project. I'd like you to step in and assist them in finishing it."

Paula liked her manager and it was her nature to help whenever possible. She was also certain that she could build a program that would increase product knowledge on the core products and improve the sales team's ability to overcome the three most frequent objections they face while selling.

Over the next week, Paula met with her teammates. Together they developed a training program that the sales manager and the president loved. They stuck with the original theme, using movie titles, and incorporated the necessary substance that Paula the Professional had developed. In fact, the president was so impressed with the program, he decided to use it in all the regions in the company.

❦ ❦ ❦

Paula declined to take part in the delivery of the training and let the other two sales people do the performing. She was having success in her territory and was more comfortable in the background in situations like this. The truth is that since she wasn't big on risk taking, she saw no need to stand up in front of her peer group and potentially stumble.

Later, on her evening run, she pondered her decision to not participate in the delivery of the training. "What is it that makes me hold back?" she asked aloud as she picked the running pace up. It was a familiar pattern for Paula the Professional. She had never been a big risk taker and playing it safe had always worked for her. Focused and conservative, Paula the Professional was getting solid results in sales. This style served her well. Or did it?

Paula continued her sales growth as the weeks passed. Her business was focused on her intentions. She was an expert on all the products in the company. She could handle the major objections with skill. Her territory management knowledge was superior to anyone else on her team. She followed the exact selling steps that were introduced to her in her first week of training. Her sales were steadily growing and Paula stayed focused on her course as there appeared to be no reason to make any changes to her approach.

ᚈ ᚈ ᚈ

Later that month, the company introduced a new product to be test marketed in Paula's region. The sales manager made a major push with the team and introduced a contest that would pay double commissions to the top three people who sold the most of the new product over the next month. While the last three new products that were introduced had turned out to be solid revenue streams for the company, Paula was always apprehensive when introducing something unproven to her customer base. Therefore, she would choose to wait until this latest introduction was established in the market before releasing it to her customers. Even with the double commission opportunity, it was always better to be safe than sorry. Or was it?

With one week left in the month, the manager always posted

the sales rankings of the fifteen reps in the region. The ranking was for that specific month only, and it was a tool he used to keep the competitive spirit alive and to get that extra push to close each month. Paula was in the office on the Friday afternoon when he posted the standings. To her surprise, she had slipped to eighth place among the fifteen. Granted, there was a slim margin between her and the top seven, but she wasn't accustomed to being in eighth place with one week left. If anything, she was usually ranked in the top three and would generally finish in the top five. The reason for this month's slippage was clear: the new product had really taken off. Although she didn't show it, Paula was bothered by her decision to be so conservative once again. It's not that she was failing — in fact, far from it. Her approach had served her well to get her this far. But what if she stepped it up a little bit? What if she took a few more risks? What if she concerned herself less with failure and just went for it?

❦ ❦ ❦

She was considering these questions as she pulled into Steve's gas station to fill up and pick up a bottle of water for her evening run. She considered the difficulty in abandoning a lifetime of thinking. That would be no easy task, but maybe changing her approach slightly might be beneficial. She would think about it further on her run later that evening.

As she turned her attention to the station, she noticed that the homeless man was in position on the corner holding his sign. She knew she'd soon see Steve, and he'd likely either be thanking a customer for the business, helping someone, or keeping his station spotless. Sure enough, as she began filling her car, she saw Steve giving directions to some people who had pulled in specifically for that purpose. True to his nature, he treated them as if they were his best customers. The station was full of life. Cars lined up two deep to fuel in each of the lanes. The intermittent cycling noise of the car wash filled the air and as the mini-mart doors opened and closed, people filtered in and out.

Of course, out on the corner stood the homeless man with a cardboard sign in hand that read, "Need Money, Homeless Vet, God Bless!"

Steve finished giving directions and made his way over to Paula. "Hello, young lady. How's the world treating you today?"

Paula looked out at the homeless man and back at Steve. "How could it be bad compared to that, Steve?"

"I know what you mean. He's got to have someplace to go, though. I imagine everybody else gave him a pretty rough time until he ended up on this corner."

"He's lucky to have a nice guy like you, Steve, letting him stand there all day." Paula's comment was heartfelt.

"You know, it's funny. I made a deal with that boy. About a year ago, I told him as long as he didn't sit down and didn't bother my customers, I wouldn't give him a hard time. If he sat down, I'm afraid he'd get run over by someone. Or, he'd pass out and then he'd just be lying there and I'd have to do something. To be honest with you, I also thought that might make him go away. He must spend six hours a day standing there, and not once has he ever sat down. You got to give him credit for that."

Steve was sincere with his words, and Paula could tell that it pained Steve to witness this man's difficulties each day. He went on, "Some people give him a hard time too. Young kids will go by and yell at him. Every once in a while, someone will throw something at him and if it's garbage he makes the effort to put it in the trash can. He does manage to take in a few bucks each day though."

"Occasionally, customers will complain about him being there. I just ask them if they are really bothered by him, and if he's really hurting them, I'll make sure that he is removed from the property. Nobody's ever been able to say that he was all that much of a bother. I think they get a little embarrassed about complaining about him by the time I'm done talking." Steve gave a little laugh and shook his head as he finished. "You know how some people can be. God bless them."

At that moment, a customer pulled out of the station, rolled down the window, and gave the man some change. As the homeless man put the money in his pocket, something occurred that was contrary to what Steve had just told Paula. The man dropped to one knee, his sign left his hands, and he fell to the ground, and in a split second, he went face-first onto the pavement. He lay with his arms by his side and his head turned so that his face pointed toward Paula and Steve. His eyes were shut and vomit poured from his mouth.

A lady who must have seen the whole thing let out a scream and ran up to the man. Now on her knees, she bent down with her ear near his mouth. The woman became frantic and screamed hysterically, "He's not breathing. Somebody do something!"

People in the station moved to gather around the man. The place came to a standstill as all attention went to the crisis at hand. The woman stood up from her kneeling. That was not easy considering she was easily seventy-five pounds overweight. She had ruined the knees of her stockings. Her hysteria continued, "We need a doctor! We need a doctor! Who knows CPR? Somebody save this poor man!"

Paula couldn't believe what she was seeing. She was especially surprised at the timing of such an event. They were just talking about the homeless man, his deal with Steve, and his long hours standing and never breaking their agreement. Everything was happening so fast. Paula turned and looked at Steve. To her surprise, he was not looking out at the mayhem on the curb but was focused directly on Paula. His stare into Paula's eyes was piercing. Later she would reflect that it was as if he was reading her whole life in just a few seconds.

Without taking his eyes off of Paula, Steve calmly said these words. "What's it gonna be, Paula?"

"What?" she said in an attempt to stall and act as if she didn't know what he was talking about.

"Are you going to keep tiptoeing around the edge of the pool?

Or are you going to jump in?"

Steve's words were gentle, yet firm. He was the only one who was not in a hurry at that moment, as his attention remained locked on Paula the Professional. She realized right then that Steve knew she was trained in CPR, though she was certain that she had never told Steve. She'd spent summers during college as a lifeguard and CPR certification was a requirement for the job. She had used it twice in her four years on the job, and on both occasions she was successful in resuscitating the swimmers. Both were children and each time she had another lifeguard that she teamed with to bring them back.

"Steve, it's been a long time, and..." She was near tears as Steve interrupted her.

"Are you going to keep playing it safe, or are you going to go for it?" Steve's demeanor hadn't changed, only now he turned his back on her and began walking away. To her surprise, it was not in the direction of the fallen homeless man and the crowd of people. Instead he walked right into his mini mart.

Paula looked toward the mini mart and then out at the crowd. She did this several times as she thought about what to do. She was visibly upset by now: her bottom lip was trembling and tears welled up in her eyes. It had been so long since she'd had to use CPR. And what were the recent changes to it? If she waited just a few minutes more, the paramedics would arrive. Somebody surely would have called them by now. It would be impossible not to with the way the woman was carrying on out there.

She looked again at the crowd. Why couldn't there be a doctor or nurse on the property? To take an action that was contrary to her conservative thinking was a terrific challenge for Paula. Not just in this situation, but throughout her entire life, she hadn't been a risk taker. Not during her soccer days, not during college, and certainly not during her time in sales. "I don't do this!" she said out loud to no one but herself.

Paula the Professional closed her eyes and tried to focus on what she was going to do next. To her, it seemed that time had stood still, but only a few minutes had passed. Now her analytical skill set kicked in and in a matter of seconds, she determined that first and foremost there was a life at stake and maybe she could save it. If she failed, it would be better to have tried than done nothing at all and let the man die. She would feel terrible if she sat back and did nothing, while this poor man with almost nothing lost his life.

Again, she was thinking out loud as she said, "Fight or flee, Paula. Decide now!"

Steve watched calmly from inside the mini-mart as Paula slipped between the gas pumps, crossed an island and moved around a car and out to the crowd that had gathered at the edge of the curb around the fallen homeless man. Her fists were clenched and her arms locked at her side as she spoke with a broken voice, "Excuse me, I know CPR. Maybe I can help."

From the crowd a man said, "Everyone out of the way. Let her in!" and they made a path for her to the man on the ground.

Paula could feel everyone's eyes on her as she knelt down next to the homeless man. He hadn't moved from his initial fall. He was on his stomach with his face toward the gas station just as he had fallen. A trail of vomit from the man's mouth reeked of stale booze. His eyes were closed and his face was deathly pale.

The hysterical woman let out a loud, "Thank God you're here, dear!" And her legs wobbled as she stumbled backward. Two men reached out and caught the large woman as she fell back; it took both of them to sit her down on the ground. One of the men gave her his bottle of water.

Paula was wearing black slacks, black dress shoes and a turquoise silk blouse. As she knelt down next to the man, she gagged from the smell, as it was apparent that the man had lost all of his body fluids. Add the vomit and his overall hygiene and it didn't quite compare to her experiences as a lifeguard. Nevertheless she acted quickly. She took the man's dirty gray hat with the angry eagle on it off of his head. She reached her hand into the man's mouth and cleared the vomit from his throat. She quickly wiped her hand on her pants. She turned the man over on his back, tilted his head back and confirmed that he wasn't breathing. She found that he had a pulse, though it was very faint.

Paula pinched the man's nose and without hesitation placed her mouth over the top of his. With that, some in the crowd groaned. The man's chest rose as she blew into his mouth. She did this twice, sat back and counted to four, and was ready again at five. She repeated this process for what seemed like forever, but was really just long minutes. He still wasn't breathing on his own.

"Come on, man. Breathe!" Paula said through gritted teeth. "Give it to me!"

Just then the hysterical heavy woman said, "You keep it up, sweetie! You can do it!" She then looked up at one of the men she was leaning against and breathed, "I need more water."

Paula continued her efforts. Sweat dripped from her face. Just as she was about to blow into his mouth again, the homeless veteran let out a cough. Paula turned her head just in time as vomit hit the side of her face and her hair. Acting quickly, she turned the man's face to the side as he began to cough and dry heave. The crowd, which by now had grown to some twenty people, let out a huge cheer. At that moment, two paramedics appeared and knelt down beside Paula and took over. Later she would recall that she had never even heard the ambulance siren.

Paula sat back on the ground with her knees up and feet on the ground. She leaned back on her hands. The crowd, knowing the drama was over, began to disperse. As people left, they patted Paula on the shoulder and made comments like, "Good job! Nice work! Way to step up!" Paula sat expressionless on the ground and looked straight ahead. She was a mess. Sweaty, smelly, vomit in her hair and on her face, shoes scuffed, and holes in the knees of her slacks.

Then Steve appeared at her side with a damp towel. He wiped

her face and eyes and cleaned the vomit from her hair as best he could. She leaned over and hugged onto him tightly and began to sob. She had to let it go.

"Tell me what you are feeling right now," Steve said to her as she hugged him. "You just did something that was completely out of character for you. It could have gone either way and that man could have died while you were trying to save him. But you made a decision to take a risk even though you could have sat back and waited for the paramedics to arrive. You didn't have to do what you did. Tell me what you are feeling."

Paula looked up at the old man, "I'm not sure exactly how I feel. I'm happy that it turned out well. I want you to know that I didn't hesitate because of who he is. It's just that it was a long time ago that I got certified for CPR. It's not like me to just leap into things. I could have failed at performing CPR correctly. He could have died right in front of me."

"And how would you have felt if you had done nothing?" Steve was asking the hard questions. "You know what, Paula? You don't have to answer that. No more questions today from me. You've been through a lot and you did great." Steve handed Paula the bottle of water she was going to buy and helped her to her feet.

"Thanks Steve," she said as she began collecting herself. She took the towel from Steve and further wiped her face and cleaned her hands off. She opened the bottle of water, filled her mouth and used it like mouthwash as she spit it out to the side. Once a jock, always a jock.

The paramedics loaded the homeless veteran into the ambulance. One of them came back and talked to Paula. "Are you okay?"

Paula was standing now, "I'm fine. How's he doing?" she asked.

"It looks like he was severely dehydrated. We're going to take care of him. We see this kind of thing all the time. Usually though, there isn't someone like you around. You saved that man's life."

"It was nothing," Paula said dryly. "I never gave it a second thought." She was being facetious.

"The world needs more people like you."

He reached out and they shook hands and he moved quickly back to the ambulance where the homeless man was strapped in and ready to go.

"If you only knew," she said quietly under her breath.

The other paramedic was seeing to the hysterical woman who was sitting and fanning herself with her hand. Obviously fine, he helped her up and she went over and sat on a bench outside the mini-mart. He ran to the ambulance, jumped in the passenger seat and the two paramedics and the homeless man roared off to the hospital.

Steve had gone back to doing what he does. He was washing the front window of an old lady's car as Paula walked over to the restroom, went inside and washed her hands and face with soap and water. Before she reached for the paper towels, she looked in the mirror above the sink and said sarcastically to herself, "You look great, Paula." She used the paper towels and went outside and got into her car, which Steve had moved to a parking spot during the commotion. She looked over and saw there was a case of her favorite water on the passenger seat. "Steve," she said as she began to pull out of the station. As she was leaving the driveway, she paused and looked where the homeless man would normally be standing.

☙ ☙ ☙

Overall, she was glad that she had taken action. The man was alive and the ordeal was over. Tonight, she would pass on her evening run.

The first thing that Paula did when she got home was brush her teeth, throw the toothbrush away and replace it with a new one in the holder. After a long hot shower, Paula slipped on some sweats and an old soccer t-shirt and went out to the kitchen to eat a light dinner. Taped on her refrigerator were her intentions. Although she'd seen them hundreds of times, she looked at them as if it were the first time.

I intend to be an expert in all of our products

I intend to be an expert at overcoming the key objections

I intend to be an expert at following our selling steps

I intend to be an expert at territory management

I intend to work hard and turn this knowledge into sales

I intend to earn well into six figures this year

She nodded her head in agreement as she completed reading each line. At this moment she realized that she was missing something in her business intentions—a key that could help her accelerate. She remembered the questions that she was asking herself before she saved the man's life.

She repeated what she was thinking earlier in the day. "What if I stepped it up a little bit? What if I took more risks? What if I concerned myself less with failure and just went for it? How would I feel and what kind of results would I get?"

Today's events at the gas station had Paula considering changing her approach to her life. That thought alone was both amazing and somewhat frightening to Paula the Professional. Here was a woman who had been successful at each of the things that were passionate to her. As an athlete, she played on an elite team that was the number one team in the nation. As a student, when she finally committed to being successful, her improvement in the classroom was remarkable. In sales, she had become a top producer by being fundamentally sound in all areas of her job. Yet while her feelings were not unlike the feelings of uneasiness that she had been experiencing, tonight they were much greater than ever in the past. There was more for Paula the Professional and she knew it. What exactly was she on to?

She thought about her decision to help the homeless man today. What would have happened had she not been able to bring him back? Tough question. But she knew she would have done everything she could do and the paramedics would have taken over. At least she would have tried. Reflecting on it now, she realized that she would have felt terrible about herself had she not stepped in and tried to help.

How would it affect her if he hadn't made it? She considered that question and determined that she would feel bad for the man but content that she had done her best to help in that situation. The important thing to her was that she had taken action, and that action definitely helped the outcome be positive.

Why had she hesitated in the beginning? She thought about that one for a minute and decided that it was in her nature to be conservative. "I'm analytical, logical, even tempered, and patient. I'm not an extrovert. But you know what? That doesn't mean I should always play it so safe. Life is about going for it." She laughed out loud at how she had been talking to herself.

Paula the Professional had much to think about, but tonight she would end the evening feeling good about today's decision to dive into a difficult situation.

❦ ❦ ❦

During the weekend, Paula couldn't help but play Friday's scenes over and over again in her head. Doing so, she experienced several emotions. Overall, she felt gratification for taking action. She got goose bumps when she reflected on how close she came to not acting at all. Any way that she analyzed it, playing it safe and not diving in would have caused her more pain than had she failed at breathing life into the homeless man.

She was convinced that risk-free action brings predictable and certain results. After all, she had basically lived her life that way. However, perhaps too much of life goes untouched with such a conservative philosophy. But by living risk free, you lose opportunities. Maybe, the practical side of her thought, those who take occasional chances live more, grow more, and even earn more. Gradually, over the weekend, Paula reached her decision.

❦ ❦ ❦

On Monday morning, Paula reviewed her decision on the way to work. She'd adjust her thinking as she approached her selling day and move through her day with a different outlook. While she would continue to be careful not to make critical mistakes, she would be less cautious regarding small failures that could lead to future success. She would expand her cold calling efforts and not worry so much about the rejection. She would introduce the new products to her customers without hesitation. She would move quicker and try to be less analytical about unimportant details.

She would do all of this with the goal of being comfortable in her own skin. Paula the Professional had just given herself a new challenge. She would take aim and trust her skills without hesitation.

Even as a top producer, Paula the Professional had always worked within conservative parameters that left additional opportunities untouched. Additionally, there was an emotional void that existed because she always knew that she had more in her. She realized that current success and hesitation were keeping her from that next level.

"Is this what has been bothering me?" she thought. Is this the void I've been feeling? Not fear, not lack of fulfillment, but the fact that I'm missing opportunity because of my conservative nature?"

She had two hours before her first appointment and decided to head in that direction making walk-in cold calls along the way to potential customers with whom she had failed to secure appointments in the past. Paula usually relied on the telephone to secure her first appointments. But this time, with the attitude of nothing to lose and everything to gain, she would walk right into the face of high rejection and not worry about the outcome. In fact, she told herself that regardless of the outcome, it would be a positive experience because she was out there taking risks that just last week she would have never taken.

Over the course of the next hour, she made four cold calls. Two of the places made it clear that they were completely happy with

Paula's competition and didn't foresee making a change in the near future. Paula's territory management knowledge had already told her that much. However, at the third call, she was able to secure a meeting with the buyer in a month. He spoke to her for a grand total of three minutes, but he did give her an appointment.

On her fourth call, she couldn't get past the gatekeeper, but she was able to leave her card and the receptionist assured her that she would pass the card along. She did secure the name of the decision maker who happened to be the son of the owner of the business. This was new knowledge to Paula, and she knew that with new decision makers came potential change. Not a bad call.

Since she was in the area and she still had an hour before her first scheduled appointment, Paula decided to take her "don't play it so safe" thinking to a new level. She was enjoying her feeling of empowerment as she pulled right in front of the next call. She sat in her car and looked up at the business. Before her was the establishment where she had experienced "the worst sales call of my life" two years ago. She had never been back and now she was actually considering walking through the doors of the business in front of her. Inside was the man who had given her an appointment for the specific purpose of shredding her for something that she had nothing to do with.

She sat in the car and weighed her feelings on this one. What was the worst thing that could happen? She concluded that the odds were good that the man would conduct himself the same way he did two years ago. How painful would that really be? She'd been reliving it all this time anyway; it couldn't be any harder. What's worse, getting roughed up by a bully, or driving by this opportunity once per week and not taking action? She nodded her head as she concluded that no action was the worse thing she could do.

Paula the Professional was proud of herself for her new thinking. She'd always had a strong work ethic, always had been an achiever, but now she was about to add an additional tool to her toolbox. She was going to take some risks that, just days before, she'd have considered unthinkable.

She entered the building, introduced herself to the receptionist and requested a few minutes with the owner. The receptionist made a call and told Paula that he was very busy but if she could wait for a little while, he'd give her five minutes.

Paula considered excusing herself or asking for an appointment at a later date, but instead said, "That will be fine. Thank you very much."

As she sat in the lobby, she had no idea what she was going to say to the owner, which by itself was completely out of character for Paula the Professional. She quickly pulled a plan together based on some assumptions about his behavior. Whichever way he acted, Paula was semi-prepared. She didn't feel perfect about things, but was grateful to be playing at a new level that she wouldn't even have considered last week. After all, there was a good chance that he'd make it short and sweet. Well…short, anyway.

The receptionist was busy taking calls and after fifteen minutes she said to Paula, "He'll see you now. Go through those doors, turn right and go to the end of the hall. It's the last door on the left. Have you been here before?"

"Thank you. Yes, I have." Paula said, somewhat disbelieving that she was actually doing this. "I know right where it is." With that, Paula the Professional headed through the automatic doors, turned right, went to the end of the hall, turned left and right into the owner's den. She wondered if the people she passed on the way could hear her heart pounding.

Sitting behind a giant U-shaped desk in his very large office, sat the man who had released all of his anger on Paula the Professional two years earlier.

"I'll say this much for you, kid. You got guts," boomed the voice from behind the desk.

"Good morning, and thank you for seeing me. I'm Paula…" She was determined not to let him see her sweat.

He interrupted, "Yeah, I know who you are. Look, let me save you some time. Nothing has changed on my end." His demeanor was the same angry man that he was two years ago. "Like I told you the last time you were in here, when I did business with you guys, I got completely screwed. I don't make the same mistakes twice. I'd be out of business if I did."

Paula the Professional looked directly at the man who had ripped her up the last time they were in this situation. She was going to take a risk with her words. "If I may say so, I don't make the same mistakes twice either. That's why I'm here. In the past two years I've gained more market share than any other competing company. And guess where I got that market share? From them! Additionally, our company has been completely revamped since your last experience with us. The sales rep—that's me—and management are completely different. We have third-party research that shows our product line is superior to that of our major competitors. People in your exact situation—your competitors, to be specific—are taking advantage of what we have to offer. I have the testimonials to prove it. I want your business and frankly, sir, I'm not the rep who screwed you. I'm Paula and my customers trust me. You should call some of them. I'd be happy to give you references."

Paula's tone never changed. She spoke professionally and her demeanor was sincere and confident. In her life, she had never been this assertive with a prospect, but in this case, she had absolutely nothing to lose.

Silence filled the room as they stared at each other. Paula the Professional was smiling as she always did. She wasn't about to speak again until he did. The best sales people in the world talk less than their customers and she'd said enough. It was time to wait and see.

The owner looked at her as he considered his next words. After what felt like an eternity to Paula, he said, "I appreciate that you didn't have anything to do with my past dealings with your company. I'll tell you this much, if I were ever to consider doing business with you guys, I'd want some consideration for the past and I'd want to meet your boss. I'm a damn big account for anybody, you know."

Paula could not believe she was hearing buying signals. She knew exactly what to do in this situation. Everything she had always done in the past. She was Paula the Professional. "I'm sure that my boss would like to meet you and I know we can work something out for the past. He's a very creative guy."

"We'll see about that. Here's where I'm at. I have two contracts expiring in ninety days. I'll take a look at what you have to offer and we can go from there. See me in thirty days and I'll take a look at your product."

A good sales person knows when to get out, and this was the time. "That would be great. I won't bring my manager with me until we're further along, but I will make him aware of our conversation. Can I schedule our meeting right now?"

"Give me a call in a couple of weeks and I'll put you on my calendar."

"Good enough. Thanks for seeing me today." Paula handed him her business card, reached out and shook his hand, and headed for the door.

"Thanks for coming by," said the man from behind his desk.

"Thank you for seeing me."

Paula floated down the hall, through the doors, out into the lobby where she thanked the receptionist. On the way out to her car, she wondered how much more business was in her territory if she continued to be less cautious and take more risks.

"Are they risks or are they opportunities?" She said to herself in the car. The answer was becoming clear to Paula the Professional.

After her next appointment and a quick lunch, she devoted the rest of her day to her face-to-face cold calling efforts. She made five calls and was completely rejected in four of them. She did get the names of two new contacts that she would input into her territory management plan later. And with that one call she secured an appointment for two weeks from now.

ǂ ǂ ǂ

Later that evening Paula reviewed her day. She really had made only one change. She had decided to be less concerned with "playing it safe" in her selling. She discovered that even though she had a strong work ethic, and even though she was one of her team's top producers, there existed additional opportunity if she accepted small failures in her quest for growth, took some risks, and just went for it. Being the logical person that she is, she decided to continue in this mode for the rest of the week and evaluate her progress at that time.

ǂ ǂ ǂ

At week's end, Paula was mentally and physically drained. At the same time, she felt a sense of fulfillment that she had unknowingly been longing for. Her past aggravations and uneasiness, although subtle when present, were directly attributed to her decision to approach life so conservatively. While Paula the Professional would never deviate far from what had brought her this far, a slight change not only held the promise of escalated success, but also felt very invigorating. She had played the game this week on a new level and felt a sense of fulfillment that had been so fleeting in the past.

At the end of the day Paula the Professional, a slightly changed woman, was en route to get gas before enjoying a relaxing weekend. She reflected on how she had arrived at this new state of mind. She knew it started with her decision to help the homeless man. The chain of events that day had been so remarkable it almost seemed staged by Steve. But that was not only illogical; it was almost impossible. She smiled to herself as she pulled into the station.

Steve was busy hosing down the property one section at a time. It was obvious why this busy gas station looked brand-new at all times. Steve took pride in providing the public with a good product. He waved to customers as they pulled in and out of the station. "Wal-Mart is missing a greeter," she thought to herself.

Paula began pumping her gas. Steve saw her, moved his hose over to the side so nobody would run over the nozzle, and walked over to talk to her. "There's the hero!" Steve said with that grin that he always had.

"Knock it off, Steve." Paula felt a little embarrassed considering the events leading up to her decision to jump in and help. "How are you?" she said.

"Couldn't be better, Paula. I understand that our homeless friend made it through." Steve was pleased to report the good news. Before Paula could speak, he continued, saying, "You were really terrific. A lot of my customers have asked me about you. That took a lot of guts."

Paula topped off her tank and said, "Oh, well thank you, Steve, for the push. I probably wouldn't have felt very good about myself if I had taken no action. Today though, just some gas would be fine." They both laughed. Paula added, "Thanks for the case of water. You didn't have to do that."

"It was my pleasure," Steve said. "Can't really get anywhere in life without taking some chances. Sometimes things go your way and sometimes they don't. But you never know unless you try. Sometimes not trying at all hurts a lot more than trying. Everybody needs a little push once in a while. Thanks again, for helping out." With that, Steve noticed that his display of motor oil needed to be filled. "Have a nice weekend, Paula, and thanks for the business."

Paula said goodbye to Steve and headed home for her evening run. When she was through, she stretched in her usual manner but before she showered she sat down at her computer and opened her "Intentions" file. She made this addition:

I intend to fail my way to success

She hit the printer and made three copies. With intentions in hand, she went into her bathroom, removed her old intention list and replaced it with the new one that contained the addition she had just made. She did the same thing in her home office and on her refrigerator.

I intend to be an expert in all of our products

I intend to be an expert at overcoming the key objections

I intend to be an expert at following our selling steps

I intend to be an expert at territory management

I intend to work hard and turn this knowledge into sales

I intend to earn well into six figures this year

I intend to fail my way to success

Paula's intentions had changed slightly as had her behavior this past week. She would have this new intention serve as a reminder that taking risks and handling the small failures that can lead to big successes is the key to her continued sales growth, and perhaps much more.

Chapter

4

CRAIG THE CARETAKER

Craig the Caretaker hated Monday mornings. After fifteen years in sales, it was his experience that Mondays were poor selling days because customers were preoccupied with shaking the weekend off and consumed with the challenges of the week ahead. Craig had surmised several years ago that since he was that way, it was logical that the rest of the world was similar. Therefore, he chose to give the world some "adjustment time" as he eased into each of his weeks.

On this Monday morning, Craig the Caretaker poured himself some coffee in the break room before making his way back to his desk. He sat in the middle of a bullpen area that one of the senior managers had named the "Arena" in an effort to keep the intensity running high. He was one of a hundred sales people who spent their days taking inbound calls from leads generated by targeted ad campaigns and making outbound calls to potential prospects.

It was by many standards a terrific sales position. Not only were you given leads from potential customers who were interested in your programs, the income opportunity was also well into six figures if your close rate was among the best. Of course, in order to accomplish this, you had to put in many focused hours, have a disciplined mind-set and a hunger to constantly improve in a marketplace that was ever-changing. Said differently, there were big dollars available for the best.

To people like Craig, whose resume included his share of sales positions over the past fifteen years, it was a great sales opportunity. He'd been with this company for the past two years and had put together some pretty solid months on more than a few occasions. He would have liked to have been more consistent from month to month, as his sales manager would remind him, but this was sales. Craig always felt sales could be very unpredictable.

"Sometimes you just have bad months and there's nothing you can do about it," he had said on more than one occasion to those who would listen.

On the way back to his desk, he stopped and visited with other sales reps. He had to be careful because many of them didn't buy into his theory about Mondays. They were the ones fully engaged in the assault on their week.

"They'll learn," he once said to a fellow Caretaker.

The company occupied an entire office building with two large floors totaling over one hundred thousand square feet. All the sales people, along with their managers, filled the top floor. The highest producers over time had nicer cubicles, in which one wall was a window overlooking beautiful grounds with a landscaped lawn, trees, and ponds. From their windows, the producers could even see the company's outdoor eating area that rivaled the finest of picnic areas; it was where people took breaks and ate their lunches during the warm months. It was also where the company held its monthly mixers during the summer. But rain or shine, the company was consistent: one Friday each month, the company had a mixer starting at three o'clock and all employees would enjoy a live band, food, and refreshments.

Craig the Caretaker felt that he deserved one of those nicer work areas, but he wasn't going to directly tell his manager that. Even though the sales people in those cubes were in the top twenty-five in the company, and were Performers and Professionals, he had always felt that certain managers favored certain people and that was the reason they got those spots. After all, some of the people who were already sitting in the nice offices had come into the company after Craig.

"It doesn't matter. I've been in sales a long time and my paycheck is way more important than a nice office," Craig had said to fellow Caretakers.

Craig was always in the office by eight o'clock in the morning. He prided himself on being on time. His Monday morning began with stopping at the front desk to visit with the three receptionists who in about an hour would be barraged with incoming phone calls. Ten minutes later he went to his cubicle where he would log on, get up and get some coffee, read the latest news on the Internet, and take care of his personal finances by paying some bills. Then he'd feed his tremendous personal e-mail habit that was purely social and included family, friends, and business associates in his current and past positions. After that, he would respond to his business e-mail.

By the time he had gotten his second cup of coffee and socialized his way back to his desk, it was nearly ten o'clock. That wasn't a problem for Craig or the people in the office with whom he spent his time. It was Monday morning and Mondays were a poor time to be selling. Craig would strike on Tuesday when the selling climate was better. He would spend today making sure he was ready to sell on Tuesday. He had a one-on-one meeting with his manager at two o'clock, at which time he would turn in his forecast for the month. He still had to put that together. He also had some operational issues that he had to deal with regarding a few of his deals. And he had to prioritize his existing leads.

At lunchtime he had to run some personal errands that he hadn't taken care of on the weekend. For obvious reasons related to his thinking, Craig the Caretaker took longer lunches on Mondays. As he was walking out of the "Arena" and toward the stairs, his sales manager caught up to him to discuss their meeting later that day.

"Craig, before our meeting this afternoon, I'd like you to think about something. Since you've joined the company, your production has been fairly inconsistent. Don't get me wrong; you've had some great months, even as recently as two months ago. I know we've talked about this before, but I'd like you to think about how you can produce at that higher level consistently instead of having a good month only every third month. If you did that, your sales and your income would go way up."

"Will do," Craig the Caretaker said with that polite grin he gets when he's having other thoughts.

༅ ༅ ༅

Craig ran his errands in an hour and was making his last stop for some gas before heading back to the office. He pulled into Steve's gas station where he had been getting gas for the last five years. He had first discovered Steve's station when he and his family relocated to that side of town.

They had lived in a bigger house in a more expensive neighborhood, but Craig grew tired of the pressure of making those big house payments. "You never know when this sales run could end, and I don't want to get caught with these big expenses," he had said at the time. He and the family had decided to downsize to take the pressure off. Although he would never admit it, Craig didn't feel right about that decision. His peers who had remained with his former company had continued to excel. Craig never talked about that to anyone, but inside he was bothered by his decision.

As he was pumping his gas, he thought about his upcoming meeting at two o'clock with the boss. He couldn't count the number of meetings he'd had with bosses in the last five years over his consistency—or what they'd call his lack of consistency. "More, more, more," he said softly as he looked at the nozzle pumping the fuel into his tank. "It's never enough."

Steve was just finishing washing the front window of his minimart. Craig thought about Steve, his age, the fact that he was still in business, and couldn't understand why Steve didn't hire somebody to do the day-to-day work, or sell the business outright. Just then, Steve looked over and gave Craig a grin and a nod with his head. As Craig waved back to Steve, he thought about the timing of their exchange. It was as if Steve heard what Craig had thought about hiring a window washer.

Steve coiled up his hose, set it to the side and walked over to Craig the Caretaker. For an eighty-year-old man, Steve was in great physical condition. In fact, Craig suddenly realized, Steve looked to be in better shape than he was. Now that was depressing.

"Steve, you look great, man," he said to the gas station owner. "How do you stay so fit?"

"Good to see you, Craig. Thanks for coming in." Steve never forgot to thank his customers for the business. He was so sincere that he had a way of making people feel good about themselves. Craig thought about how he had that skill too, but things have changed so much that it isn't as important in the world today. Of course, Craig had many opinions.

"Steve, they say that as we age we produce less testosterone. As time passes, it's more and more difficult to keep muscle on and easier to gain fat. But you seem to break that rule." Craig the Caretaker was well versed in many areas.

"Well," Steve said, "I'm not in as good as shape as I used to be. You know, Father Time and all. But I've heard something about that testosterone and I just never let my mind buy into it. I have a pretty strict exercise program that I've modified over the years. I stay active, and I watch what I eat. I'm not what I used to be. Don't hear as well, don't see as well, stand a little crooked. But it'll do."

"I watch what I eat too, Steve. All the way into my mouth," and they both laughed at Craig's exaggerated delivery of the old joke.

Whenever Steve saw Craig, he was reminded of how easy it was to like him. He was always cordial and upbeat; he always felt that Craig had great people skills that could take him a long way. "So tell me, a salesman like you must be knocking them dead month after month. How's it going?"

Craig was slightly surprised at the coincidence of Steve's "month after month" phrasing. Truthfully, after the vibe he got from his manager this morning, he wasn't quite sure how it was going but he wasn't going to let on. Meetings like the one coming up with his boss always made him nervous.

"It's going well. I should have a great month. It's never enough, though. They always want more. I deliver a great month and they want me to keep doing it. I've been around long enough, Steve, to know that it's just part of the game."

"Who's they?" Steve said.

"Huh?"

"They! Who are you talking about?"

Craig looked at Steve, puzzled by his question. "You know. The boss, the company. They!"

"Aren't you all one team?"

"Well, yeah. No. Kind of."

Steve then broke out into a grin like he had been kidding Craig.

"Cut it out, Steve. Let a man get some gas."

"You know," Steve said as he looked out at the traffic in the street, "I like to watch that National Geographic channel and I happened to see a special the other night on the cheetah."

Craig the Caretaker didn't know where this one was going.

"Anyway, that cat is really something. They have the chassis of a greyhound." Steve was an old car guy.

"Man, they are built for speed. Light boned, swaybacked," as he reached out with a flat hand and palm down, tracing the air in the shape of Cheetah's back. "They can get up to seventy miles per hour. Can you imagine that?"

Now Craig was puzzled and started thinking about his meeting coming up.

"I'll make this quick, Craig. I know you have a meeting to go to," Steve said. Craig wondered silently: just how did Steve know that?

"This special was filmed in Kenya. It was all about how the cheetah hunts the antelope herd. See, they try to get within fifty yards of these guys. It's ideal when they have the available cover to hide in. Like any cat, they wait in that crouched position." Now Steve quickly went in and out of a crouching position to demonstrate what he was talking about.

Craig bit his lower lip so that he wouldn't laugh out loud.

"They look for a herd that is grazing and basically they wait for an antelope to venture away from the perimeter of the herd. Once that occurs and they're within fifty yards of the cheetah, then it's on. They run that antelope down by tripping it or knocking it off balance with a swipe to its back legs or rear end," and Steve made a swipe through the air like a cat.

"Once they have that thing down, they put a vice-like grip on its throat and choke it to death. It only takes a few minutes."

"Steve!" Craig was getting a little impatient and Steve was really into it. "Where are you going here? I have a meeting with my boss."

"I know you do. It just occurs to me that the antelope that gets caught by one of those rascals must not be thinking too clearly. Antelopes must have been taught not to venture away from the herd. And if they looked around, they'd probably find that the strongest, smartest, and oldest members of the herd are right smack dab in the middle of the pack. I bet they were even warned by the other antelopes about venturing off like that. Maybe they thought they had a better plan and they were smarter and faster than they really were. Or, that they were different from the rest. Maybe they were just plain hardheaded or just didn't care and wouldn't change. You know, I don't care what part of the animal kingdom you are; you can't afford to get too comfortable out there. I just find it interesting is all. Anyway, I know you have to run."

Just then a car horn honked and Steve looked over and saw one of his customers who obviously wanted to talk to him. "We both have to go. It's good to see you, Craig. Hope the rest of your day goes well."

"See you next time, Steve," Craig said with a grin as he shook his head and got in his car. He was perplexed by that last conversation.

"What's the old man talking about now?" he thought.

Craig the Caretaker arrived back at the office in time to slap together his forecast for his meeting with his sales manager. On the drive back, he probably should have been thinking about his upcoming meeting, especially since his manager made it clear that she wanted to talk about his lack of consistency. Instead he thought about Steve's story. The cheetah, the antelope herd, the straying antelope, the kill. Huh? What was the old man talking about?

"He should have retired a long time ago," he said to himself as he walked up the stairs.

ジ ジ ジ

Craig was in his sales manager's office at two o'clock sharp. She was concluding a phone call and signaled for him to take a seat in one of the two chairs in front of her desk. A large nicely framed picture was hanging on the wall directly behind her. It showed a woman in the desert standing on top of the tallest rock surrounded by other smaller rocks. The rock must have been three hundred feet high and the woman looked like an experienced rock climber dressed in the appropriate gear. The sun was just coming up, as she stood covered in sweat with her eyes closed as she faced the new day. The caption at the bottom of the picture read, "Success is No Accident."

The sales manager hung the phone up and handed Craig the Caretaker a single sheet of paper. "I'll get right to the point, Craig. I think you have tremendous skill, but I question your heart. Your production is telling a story that we need to discuss."

Craig immediately interrupted and defensively said, "Aren't I here on time every day?"

The sales manager leaned forward. "Yes, you are, Craig. But before you speak, please let me finish."

Craig sat back in his chair as he found himself back in a familiar place.

"This discussion is not going to be about your strengths. It is my intention, as your manager, to tell you exactly what I believe is holding you back from increasing your sales. It will be your decision as to how you choose to receive this. I have only one goal and that is to help you break through your inconsistency."

Craig gave it another shot with, "But if you look at my year-to-date numbers, I'm not doing too badly."

The sales manager's demeanor went unchanged as she restated her position. "Craig, let me talk for a minute. At the end we'll have a discussion. And again, my intentions are to help you. I want to make sure that you hear me."

Now Craig flashed that smile that he's been known to use when he is silently protesting and said, "Okay."

"Thank you," the sales manager said genuinely. "I believe that inside you is a tremendous producer, and I also believe that you are completely stuck in a comfort zone. I'd like to tell you how I define the term 'comfort zone.' I use a simple formula. It starts with your personal motivation."

The sales manager went on to explain that the greater the personal motivation, the greater the opportunity to achieve at a high rate, and vice versa.

"And, I believe that your personal motivation is not that great.

Therefore, it is difficult to achieve at a high rate month in and month out. Simply put, you are motivated to do well about every third month. At least, that's what the numbers are telling me."

This time Craig the Caretaker did not attempt to interject.

"Additionally," the sales manager continued, "your sales are a result of how much focused attention you apply to your personal motivation." She told Craig that without focused attention, personal motivation is just a dream and that both ingredients are required to achieve consistently high results.

"It is my personal observation that you focus during only part of your week." She emphasized "part" as she spoke.

Craig nodded his head in apparent agreement, but inside he was feeling the opposite. He thought about how many times he'd heard this one in the past. Still, he was honoring her request to listen and to respond when she was finished.

"This, Craig, is why I believe that you are in a comfort zone." The sales manager was being honest as she delivered her opinion more carefully than many of Craig's past bosses. "Whether you are stuck in that zone or not remains to be seen, and is completely up to you. I wanted to point it out to you in hopes of helping you break your pattern of mediocrity."

The word "mediocrity" stung Craig's ego as the sales manager leaned further into Craig's space and said softly, "That is why I began this discussion suggesting that you have skill but lack the heart to be a top producer. My opinion, which is supported by the numbers and my observation of your effort, leads me to believe that you are just 'Caretaking' the business."

They both sat looking at each other and Craig finally said, "I guess I can talk now."

"Please," the sales manager said as she sat back in her chair.

"Let me start by saying I am going to have a great month this month," and he slid his forecast across the desk.

The sales manager was short with him. "I know, Craig. You've had two lousy months in a row. It's your pattern." She pointed to the numbers as she said, "Every third month, see?"

"Now wait a minute," Craig said in a friendly way as he held a hand up. "My style is a little different. Now, I don't take as many calls as the rest of the team. I'll give you that. But I spend a lot of time cultivating my customers once I determine that I gain interest from them."

The sales manager had heard it from Craig before on many occasions. She wondered at that moment if it was even possible for Craig to consider changing.

Craig continued to pontificate, "Last year was my first year in this business, and I did fairly well. I'm also tracking ahead of last year at this point."

His sales manager was having trouble sitting in her seat and had to interject. "So, what you're telling me is that you're satisfied with where you are." She was incredible at keeping her cool.

"No, I'm not saying that. I'm not satisfied and I'd like to do more. I'd always like to do more."

"Then what is your point, Craig? I mean, do you agree, or disagree with what I've said and shown you here today?"

Craig the Caretaker was running out of objections but he was like a train on a track with his thinking, a man stuck in his own head.

"I agree with some of what you said today, but I want you to know that I am very motivated to be here. While it may look like a pattern, and there is some truth to that, there is good reason for my up-and-down months. For example, last October where my numbers start to dip..."

The sales manager had listened to all that she could stand and still maintain her composure. "Hang on just a second," she said as she stood up and went to her white board, which was hanging on the wall and enclosed behind cherrywood doors.

"Sure," Craig said as he turned in his chair to face the white board. "Now what? I've heard it all before," he thought to himself.

She had anticipated a struggle with Craig the Caretaker and his apparent unwillingness to change his thinking. She opened the doors to her white board to reveal the description of a Caretaker written in bullet points. It read:

- They're stuck in a comfort zone

- They don't do the difficult things

- They hate change

- They're passive-aggressive

- They're inconsistent producers — or consistently mediocre producers

- They're a sleeping Performer or Professional

"Do me a favor, Craig." She had mentally gathered herself and was back to her zone. "This is the definition of the Caretaker. I have to go to another meeting. Please take a moment to read it. Write it down if you'd like."

She stepped away from the white board and picked up a file on her desk. "Let me be clear. I believe that you are a Caretaker and nothing that we have discussed today has caused me to change my thinking. In fact, it has only strengthened my opinion. I want to be sure you get two things from this meeting."

She moved over to the door, put her hand on the knob, and turned to face Craig. "First, I firmly believe that you are stuck in a comfort zone and that is your key problem. Second, I believe you have the potential to be a top producer," and she walked over and grabbed a red marker and circled the bullet point that read, "They're a sleeping Performer or Professional." Then, as she opened the door to leave, she said, "Please think about our meeting here today," and left before Craig could respond.

"I sure will," Craig said to an empty room. "I'll leave my forecast on your desk," and this time his usual "boss" smile had a hint of sadness. Before he left, he wrote down the Caretaker definitions on his yellow pad. Then he stood up and closed the white board, hoping to avoid any embarrassment from someone reading it while he was in the room.

Craig the Caretaker went back to his cube and decided that it was time for a break after that intense session with his manager. He put his yellow pad face down on the desk and walked down the stairs and outside to the eating area. He knew that he was in no real trouble with his manager or any real danger of losing his job. After all, his numbers were good enough and he'd seen trouble in the past. This was no time for major concern.

༐ ༐ ༐

Since it was later in the afternoon, only people on their breaks occupied the lunch area. A few were in the designated smoking area furthering their commitment to death. Craig the Caretaker wasn't a smoker and he made his way over to a corner table where two sales people were sitting and talking. It was no coincidence that Caretakers tended to pack together. After all, Performers and Professionals were fully engaged in the business and didn't have as much free time. The "Pity Party" was about to begin.

"My man," said the first Caretaker as he reached out and they slapped hands. "Where have you been?"

"I was having my monthly one-on-one with the Queen." Passive-aggressive Craig the Caretaker was coming out. "The woman can make some unreasonable demands. She needs to take another look at that March I threw up. Those were some serious numbers."

At that point the second Caretaker chimed in, "I'm looking to have a month like that this month. It would be a slam dunk if our pricing was better."

"What'd she say?" the first Caretaker piped back in. It wasn't that he was so interested. He just wanted to know if there was any trouble ahead for him.

"You know, it was a lot of the usual. Give me more production.

Get more consistent. Don't get in a comfort zone." He went on to voice his complaints to the "Pity Party" about being underappreciated.

"When's the last time she sold anything, anyway?" said the second Caretaker.

The three Caretakers spent the next ten minutes protesting the unreasonable demands being made by management, criticizing everyone in authority, discussing what the programs they were selling were missing and accepting no responsibility for their mediocre performance.

In typical Caretaker fashion, Craig looked at his two partners and said, "Well, this day is about shot." He went on to explain that Mondays were not good selling days anyway and since it was three o'clock, there wasn't much left to do on this day.

"I hear you, Craig," said the first Caretaker, and with that, the three of them walked into the building and up the stairs.

❦ ❦ ❦

Back in his cube, Craig flipped over the yellow pad on which he'd written the definition of the Caretaker. He carefully looked at each of the bullet points. The first one read:

• They're stuck in a comfort zone

Craig thought about the conversation that they had about this topic and agreed that the formula of personal motivation plus focused attention was as good as any he had heard over his years. He believed that there might be some merit to what his boss was saying but he wasn't about to make any major changes.

The second bullet point was:

• They don't do the difficult things

While he wasn't exactly sure what she was talking about, he did agree that his approach to the business didn't encompass all of the fundamentals that he once used. There was a time that he would pursue the most difficult of customers provided they had a real need and his program was a solution to that need. He tended to look for easier paths these days.

The next bullet point said:

• They hate change

"I really don't see a major reason to change," he thought to himself. Craig considered the job he was doing, his upcoming month, his track record, and felt things were going just fine.

• They're passive-aggressive

That statement bothered Craig. He had just visited with his friends in the business and spent the majority of the time criticizing his manager and the company. In Craig the Caretaker's mind though, he wasn't about to voice his real feelings for fear of being fired. Besides, he felt his manager's observations were greatly exaggerated.

• They're inconsistent producers—or consistently mediocre.

"Wait until this month," he said softly. He refused to acknowledge the words "inconsistent" and "mediocre."

The last bullet point on the Caretaker list read:

• They're a sleeping Performer or Professional

Craig knew these terms and had heard many times what Performers and Professionals were. The company had a philosophy that there were only four kinds of sales people in the world. Craig and many of his fellow sales people had tried to come up with more or less than four kinds—or even different kinds—but were unable to do so.

Craig considered himself a Performer. And he didn't feel that he was "sleeping." His understanding was that Performers were emotional, intuitive, extroverted, and impatient. He recalled that they have large egos, and usually are natural sales people. In mentally recapping what Performers were, he left out three very important characteristics. Not surprisingly, these were the characteristics that, to this point in his two years with the company, he showed only glimpses of being:

- Passionate
- Very competitive
- Top producers

Craig the Caretaker had gotten in the habit in recent years of using only those facts that helped validate his thinking. The truth is, however, that he's shown few signs of passion or competitiveness, and his track record solidifies his infrequent top-producing sales results.

Be that as it may, Craig was having none of it. He tore the page off his yellow pad and placed it in a file in his bottom left-hand drawer. He was going to focus on having the big month that he forecasted.

❦ ❦ ❦

The rest of the week was carried out in typical Caretaker fashion. He was in the office promptly at eight o'clock as usual. After his social warm-up time, which was lessened because it was not Monday, Craig would log on and began taking inbound calls. During his time on the phone, he had made only limited attempts to overcome some of the objections that were being presented to him. As a result, he wasn't able to advance many of the calls to the next stage of selling. Had he used the company's sales training in conjunction with his overall sales skills, his hit rate of calls that he could actually put into his pipeline would have been greater. Said differently, he was just picking the "low hanging fruit." That's what Caretakers do. They aren't selling, they're just Caretaking.

Since he was a talented communicator, he managed to advance enough of the calls to stay mildly busy. He got those potential customers to agree to send the necessary information required to provide a quote. It was too bad he lacked the passion and competitiveness to really turn it on. As a result, many of the "hot" leads would go unclosed because Craig the Caretaker didn't make the extra effort to advance them.

In reality, that was keeping him from consistently producing.

He was stuck in a comfort zone and therefore, would produce big numbers only when it was personally required to pay the bills. Or, during some months he would get lucky and have a lot of easy customers who demanded little time. It was "order taking" disguised as sales. His pattern of inconsistent sales production was no coincidence.

During one of his many trips to the break room, he mentioned the quality of his calls to one of his co-workers, saying, "My calls are terrible today."

A top producer, who was standing close enough to hear the comment, shot back with, "Pal, they're calling us. How bad can the calls be? The callers are already interested in our programs. You ought to try working them a little."

Craig ignored the comment, as he always did when things fit outside his comfort zone.

When he wasn't taking inbound calls, he was supposed to be making outbound calls to those leads that he had gathered during his time on the phone. Although he did make callbacks, he was far too selective with the leads that he put in the "hot" pile. Many of the other leads had potential but they required too much work for Craig the Caretaker. When he was faced with difficult objections, or an opportunity that required work on his part to further cultivate the opportunity, he would pass on the deal. Unfortunately, Craig didn't see it that way. He considered them bad leads.

The truth is, Craig the Caretaker had let his mind get lazy. In fact, he had let everything in his life get lazy. He was trapped in a life of "just getting by."

Craig the Caretaker had a lot of downtime and called things "slow" when this was occurring. He was, after all, a reactive individual and spent his time waiting for things to fall into his lap. He chose not to make proactive moves and use all the tools available for him to sell. Top producers will forward a newsworthy item via e-mail to a potential customer, send a gift to a customer they just did business with, ask for a referral, or always be cold calling out to old leads that somebody like Craig had discarded. Craig wasn't operating that way. He was stuck in a comfort zone and busy at being in the way of himself. But how comfortable was he really?

That afternoon, Craig sat in his cubicle, having one of his "slow" times. It was as if he had forgotten about the Craig of the past who, not so long ago, was a top producer himself. Back then, "slow" times hadn't existed for him. In earlier years, he had considered himself to be in the momentum business and it was his job to create a lot of it. Good things always happened when he took action and there was no such thing as "slow." But Craig the Caretaker was lost. He had forgotten about the fundamentals that he practiced when he was top producing.

While he sat and waited for calls, Craig was trolling through his files on his computer. He came across an old file and opened it. It contained his goals from when he had started with the company two years ago. The results that first year didn't come close to matching his aspirations at that time. "That's why I don't set goals," he said quietly to himself. "I never hit them anymore."

At that moment, he heard the sales woman in the next cube over talking to a potential customer. She spoke with confidence and enthusiasm. Craig picked up on the conversation in midsentence, "...and this is what I'd like you to know about me. You're on the other end of the phone and don't REALLY know me. We've only talked a couple of times and both times I've sent you the information that you've needed after we determined your needs and goals. I hope I've demonstrated to you that I am a professional in this business."

There was a pause as the sales woman listened to a response from the caller. "Well, thank you," she continued. "I want you to know that if you choose to do business with me, I will be certain to get your deal done for you. I take my job very seriously."

Another pause as she listened. "Thank you. You're very kind. I'll follow up with you tomorrow, then." She concluded the phone call with the same amount of zeal that she had when Craig first picked up on the conversation. And, curiously, Craig could almost hear that she was smiling as she spoke.

After listening to that, Craig recalled a time in his life when he was like her and how refreshing and stimulating life had been in those days. "What happened to me?" he asked softly into his headset with no one on the other end.

❧ ❧ ❧

It was customary to have a company meeting each month around mid-month to recognize the achievements of the top producers for the previous month. Management would acknowledge those individuals in operations who exceeded their operational goals. It was also a forum for senior management to communicate and interact with the troops. If it had been a banner quarter, the band and food would be top rate.

It happened to be one of those Fridays and at three o'clock all of the employees in the company, with the exception of the receptionists who had to handle the phones, gathered outside under beautiful skies for an upbeat meeting. Craig was standing in his usual spot with his fellow Caretakers as the sales management team gave out framed certificates and fun awards such as dinner for two, or tickets to local concerts, to those in sales and operations who had excelled during the previous month.

As the vice president of sales announced one of the top producers, one of the Caretakers leaned over and said to Craig, "She got lucky!"

Craig nodded his head and smiled, but inside he knew how she did it. It wasn't luck. She was committed to excelling in her career. She did the things that it took to be a top producer. Therefore, she was taking the walk up to be recognized as she had so many times in the past. Craig and the other Caretakers tended to act like that type of recognition wasn't important to them. "Just pay me and let me do my job," Craig had been known to say in the past. The other members of the Pity Party would always support Craig's position.

After the announcements and awards, people interacted and enjoyed food, drinks, and music. The week couldn't end too soon for Craig the Caretaker. He went back up to his office and gathered his things to go home for the weekend. Before he closed his brief-case, he reached into his bottom left desk drawer and pulled out the yellow sheet that had the description of the Caretaker written on it. He folded it, placed it in his briefcase and made his way out of the building to his car.

❦ ❦ ❦

On the way home, Craig was feeling mentally and physically exhausted. While he always felt fatigued at the end of a workweek, today he felt absolutely drained. As good as he had gotten about blocking out things that he didn't want to think about, he kept replaying the meeting with his sales manager that he'd had on Monday. Although he'd had meetings with sales managers that were similar to this in the past, Craig genuinely was feeling the pain of this one. It was a pain, however, that he couldn't pinpoint.

Craig was accustomed to spending time in what his fellow Caretakers called the "woodshed." This was a term that they used when management would meet privately with sales people about their lack of production. It was a familiar term taken from the old days when a boy got in trouble with his parents and the dad would take him outside to the woodshed to "correct" his behavior with physical punishment.

Craig was thinking about the many meetings with various managers over the years and their claims of his heartless efforts. Craig the Caretaker was actually considering the validity of this sales manager's claims. While it felt terrible to be classified as a Caretaker, it was becoming increasingly difficult to hide from the truth. Craig was a Caretaker—now. Of course, during his moment of self-realization, he had no recall of the part about him being a "sleeping Performer or Professional." His mind was too busy beginning to accept that he in fact fit the profile of the Caretaker.

He thought about the comfort zone again. "You call this comfortable?" he thought to himself as he drove in the discomfort of his own emotions. Craig was beginning to grow tired of just getting by.

❦ ❦ ❦

While he was driving and thinking, the light on his dashboard lit up, indicating that he needed gas. Craig groaned and muttered to himself, "What's this? Even the car needs attention now? Why does everything demand so much work?" He heaved a sigh and headed to get gas. As he was pulling into Steve's gas station, he remembered the story that Steve had told him about the cheetah and the antelope. After the week that he'd just had, Craig found that to be an interesting coincidence. He recalled the company meeting and how he and the fellow Caretakers stood at the perimeter of the festivities. The parallels to Steve's story about the fate of the antelope who occupied the outside of the herd were just too clear to gloss over, even for him.

Craig sat in his car with both hands on the steering wheel and thought about his boss. Is she the cheetah? Or, is life? Am I one of the weak antelope? Hardheaded? Do I think I'm faster and smarter than the rest?

Pulled by the need to stay in denial, he quickly discounted the whole similarity between the Caretaker and the antelope herd. He reinforced his thinking as he said, "He's an old man in a gas station. What am I thinking about here?" With that he did his best to remove the animal kingdom from his head, got out of his car, and began filling up.

The traffic at the station was at maximum Friday afternoon capacity. Cars occupied every stall and in some cases were two deep. The mini-mart and car wash were buzzing and as Craig was filling up, he looked for Steve but did not see him. A kid at the pump across from him had his stereo blaring as he washed his windows. A girl sat in the passenger side of the car bobbing to the rhythm of the song. The kid was washing the window on her side and from their gaze at each other Craig surmised that they weren't brother and sister. "Think you could turn it up a little?" he asked cynically to himself.

Craig saw Steve pop up from the other side of a car two stalls over where he was explaining something to one of his customers. It was a young mother who drove a late-model minivan. Inside the car were three young kids, two of whom were still in car seats. The other looked to be about seven years old. All three of them were asleep. Steve was explaining something to the woman when he looked over and gave Craig a familiar wave.

When Steve concluded his discussion with the mom, he walked over to Craig the Caretaker, who had just finished filling up. "These poor single moms drive around all day with their kids in the car and they don't think to check their water, or oil, or their tires. That woman's tires were as bald as Yul Brynner, and I was explaining to her how dangerous that was."

Craig the Caretaker was looking at a passionate man who cared deeply about his job and others. He was amazed at the pride Steve took in keeping his station in great condition. He was always impressed with the energy Steve would expend to go out of his way to help others. Craig reached out his hand to Steve and said, "Happy Friday, Steve. You're looking at a guy who has never been so glad to see a week end."

Steve didn't shake Craig's hand as he wiped his hands on an old rag hanging from the pocket of his uniform and said, "I don't want to get you all filthy, Craig. I got dirt all over my hands from that woman's tire. I told her where she could get a good deal on a new set." He took an extra gaze at Craig and said, "Had yourself a tough week?"

Steve began walking around Craig's car and looking down at each wheel. He was listening for a response from Craig as he bent down in a catcher's position in front of each tire. He ran his hands around the outside of each of the tires and inspected the remaining rubber.

"He's a machine," Craig thought to himself. Then he answered Steve's question with surprising honesty. "Yeah, Steve, I had a tough week. It's starting to occur to me that I may be going about this whole sales thing wrong. It always feels like I'm swimming upstream, yet I'm hardly doing any paddling."

"That sounds like a pretty interesting comment. What do you mean?" Steve was in the crouched position reaching over the top of a tire and feeling the other side.

"I mean I think it might take just as much energy to avoid doing things as it does to just do them." Craig couldn't believe he was being so open to the old man who owned a gas station.

Steve nodded his head as Craig continued, "I've spent a lot of years making sure I didn't have to work too hard, and you know, in hindsight, that can be pretty hard work in itself." Craig's voice hardened as he said, "I'm starting to wonder how I would feel if I just went for it. I mean it gets kind of mentally draining just getting by. I wonder what would happen."

"Well," Steve said, "I don't know how much easier it would be, Craig, but I do know you would feel a whole lot better about yourself if you changed your intentions a little bit."

Steve stood up and walked over to the other side of the car, opposite Craig. He started to bend down to go through the same routine of checking the tires as he said, "Not only would you feel better about yourself, but the financial reward would be kind of nice too. It seems to me that it would be a whole lot nicer in the middle of the herd with the strong antelope than looking over your shoulder all the time on the outside of the perimeter. You know what I mean?"

Craig laughed and shook his head. "I guess I knew you were talking about me when you told that story." He was looking in the direction of where Steve was but could not see him because he had bent down to check a tire. "I swear to God, Steve," Craig the Caretaker said, as he continued laughing, "sometimes..."

"Uh-oh," Steve interrupted from the other side of the car. "You better come take a look at this, Craig!"

"Wait a minute. You're not getting out of this one that easy," Craig said as he walked around his car to the other side. "Besides, there's only ten thousand miles on these tires."

Steve looked up at Craig who was standing beside him. "Come down here and take a look at this. Run your hand right here."

Craig knelt down beside Steve and put his hand on top of the tire and moved in back to meet Steve's. As he did so, he felt what seemed to be a nail sticking out of his tire. "Oh great!" he said.

"You better get that in right away," Steve said as he continued to feel around the perimeter of the tire.

Craig stood up before Steve and what he saw didn't register immediately. Two pumps over, there was an elderly lady filling up her car where the mother with her three kids in the van had been previously. Walking alongside the car, but on the other side of the lady, was a large, muscular man in a leather vest. He was moving slowly and looking into her car as he passed. The lady's passenger side window was rolled down and the man, almost without breaking stride, reached in and took the elderly lady's purse.

At that moment, the only one in the gas station who could have seen this occur was Craig the Caretaker. He quickly looked down at Steve who, to his surprise, was now kneeling on one knee and looking directly up at Craig and smiling.

Craig gave a whisper yell to Steve as he said, "Steve! That guy just stole that old lady's purse. What are you gonna do?"

To Craig's surprise, Steve was holding a cell phone when he said, "I already called 911, but they won't get here in time. That guy will be long gone with that old lady's money. What do you think we should do?"

Craig could not believe how relaxed Steve was being about this as he said to him in that same tone, "I don't know. It's your damn gas station."

Just then the thief, who was about six feet tall and must have weighed over two hundred pounds, turned and started walking right toward Craig. Since Craig had been kneeling down with Steve a few seconds earlier, the thief had not known that he would be in his exit path. At that moment, the thief must have realized that Craig had witnessed the whole thing. He gave a stutter step and a pause like he had just been shocked as he stared at Craig and continued walking away from the old lady's car and toward Craig and a kneeling Steve.

He had a bald head, a pitch-black goatee and was wearing silver wire-rimmed sunglasses. Tattoos were on each of his large shoulders. He didn't wear a shirt under his leather vest and a silver swastika dangled from a thick silver chain. Black boots with large heels must have given him two extra inches in height, and tight blue jeans covered his powerful legs.

"This is not a nice guy," Craig thought to himself.

Realizing that Craig had seen what he had done, the thief gave a psycho grin and picked up his pace. He was going to walk right by Craig's car, off of the lot and around the corner with the old lady's purse.

The elderly woman was oblivious to the whole thing as she continued pumping her gas.

From his crouched position, Steve looked up at Craig. Craig wanted to hear Steve say, "The simple thing is to just let him go, Craig. The police will get him eventually. That's a pretty big guy. It'd be kind of hard to stop him. No need to go changing your style now. Things are pretty comfortable for you. Why don't you just leave it that way? It'd be too difficult for you."

But Steve didn't speak. He just remained in his kneeling position and looked up at Craig. It wasn't a challenging look, or a concerned look, and it certainly wasn't a look of fear. It was more of a look of support. It was as if he were telling Craig that all would be okay, no matter what.

Craig was looking back and forth between Steve and the thief, who was now only twenty feet away. Craig figured that the thief's continued stare and grin were his attempts to show some intimidation and make sure that Craig wasn't getting any ideas about getting involved.

The thief had the stolen purse in his left hand down at his side as he strutted for his getaway. Apparently he was too arrogant to break out in a full sprint, even though he knew that he'd been seen. He was now ten feet and closing. In a few seconds he would be right by Steve and Craig.

Five feet away.

Now he was one step away.

Craig looked at him, undecided in his mind as to what he was going to do. Part of him thought, "Let the cops handle this."

Then the thief was even with the car and as he walked by he was startled to see Steve kneeling down behind the side of the car. With that, he came to a stop, turned and pointed his finger down at Steve as he spoke, "What are you gonna do, old man? Beat me with your tire gauge?" With that he made a step toward Steve.

Without thinking, Craig the Caretaker stepped way out of his comfort zone as he moved in front of Steve and stood toe to toe with the thief. He knew one thing at that moment. No matter what, he couldn't live with himself if he stood by and watched Steve get harmed by this psycho. It wasn't that he was so attached to Steve; it was the fact that he would have to live with taking no action. Craig had a brief flash about his life as he thought about how little action he had taken in his life these past years.

The thief laughed as he now pointed his finger directly at Craig and bounced it off of his chest as he spoke. Spit flew from his mouth, "What the hell are you gonna do, boy? I suggest you go on about your business."

As he spoke, he continued jabbing Craig's chest with his finger. The thief must have had three inches and twenty-five pounds on Craig. In addition to that, he was crazy—and crazy is always difficult to deal with.

Steve stayed in his one-knee position behind Craig as the crazy thief used his finger on Craig's chest to demonstrate his dominance.

"I've had a REALLY bad day!" Craig the Caretaker said to the thief. "In fact, I've had a REALLY bad WEEK!" With that, he took one step to his left just as the thief was making another poke with his finger. As he stepped, Craig reached up with his left hand and wrapped his hand around the thief's finger. He pulled him in the direction of the man's point, using the thief's own force against him. The thief was forced to take a step forward and to the side. This not only caused him to lose his balance, it got him away from harming Steve.

The thief had failed to account for Craig's history of on-and-off training in the martial arts. Of course, Craig had never gotten his black belt since he switched disciplines from Tai Kwan Do to Aikido to Kenpo before quitting altogether some ten years ago. Nevertheless, many of the basics from nearly four years training remained burned in his brain. But like most people who have some self-defense skill, he had never had to use any of it.

Each time that he moved to another discipline, he had his typical Caretaker excuses. "Tai Kwan Do was too much high kicking and I'm not as flexible," he had said at the time as he switched to Aikido.

"Aikido has too much throwing. I want to learn more striking techniques," he had said when he moved to Kenpo.

"There's too much sparring in Kenpo. I'm sick of getting bruised," were his final words as he left the art completely.

Craig had just used a technique on the thief that he had learned called "Borrowed Force" where you use your opponent's own force against him.

As he pulled the finger in a direction away from Steve, the thief said angrily, "I'm gonna kill you." With that, he let go of the purse and attempted a feeble swing at Craig with his free hand.

Steve reached out from his kneeling position and grabbed the purse from where it had fallen. He had a look on his face like he was being entertained as Craig the Caretaker took action that was way out of character.

Craig remained focused as he firmly bent the thief's finger back in the opposite direction that the joint is supposed to go. The thief immediately dropped to his knees and let out a screech.

"Ahhhhh! My finger, man!" the thief yelled as Craig stood over him applying pressure to the point of nearly snapping his finger.

Craig brought his other hand up to the thief's hand and twisted as he leaned back and straightened the man's arm. The thief's arm was twisted in its most unnatural position as he now lay face down on the ground. Craig stood on the man's neck and leaned back. He now had the thief completely immobilized and in the classic "Arm Bar Extension."

Craig was surprised at how the fight went out of the thief so fast. Later he would reflect on his training and the fact that, in all of the disciplines, the Sensei always discussed the weaknesses of the aggressive bully. "Don't let the illusion fool you," he recalled one saying, "Their theatrics are an expression of their fear."

The entire scene, from Craig witnessing the crime, to overtaking the thief, had taken less than two minutes. As he held the thief in submission, others in the gas station had now turned their attention to the commotion. Within minutes, a police car came screeching onto the property. The cop must have sized up the situation as he pulled onto the lot. He got out of his car, pulled his gun and pointed it down at the thief. Craig's arm bar remained intact.

"Step away immediately, sir. You, on the ground! Do not move!" The cop made it clear he was taking over.

Craig released his hold on the thief and sidestepped over to the car where Steve was now standing and holding the purse. The cop ordered the thief to put his hands behind his back as he cuffed him and sat him up. He told Craig and Steve to stay right where they were. As the cop led the thief back to his squad car, Steve noticed that the elderly lady was beginning to pull away from the pump.

She had remained oblivious to the entire incident, never even noticing the altercation between Craig and the thief. Steve handed the purse to Craig and, against the cop's orders of staying put, trotted over and spoke to the woman before she could leave. She put her hand over her heart in shock as she looked down at the seat where her purse was supposed to be. As Steve pointed out where Craig was, Craig smiled and held up the purse. Steve directed the lady to a parking spot, she pulled into it and Steve escorted her over to the scene. As they walked, Steve told her the entire story and when she reached Craig, she gave him a hug and thanked him for his courage.

The cop finished on his radio, got the complete story from Craig and Steve, and told the lady that she needed to come down to the police station to make a report. Knowing how flustered and upset she was, Steve offered to drive her.

As he began walking the lady over to his pickup, Steve turned to Craig and said, "I've got some really good news. It was only a small screw. Didn't even puncture anything. It was right between the grooves on the tread. You got lucky there, Craig," and he reached out and handed the screw to Craig.

Craig, still shocked by the whole turn of events, looked down at the screw in his open palm and then looked up at Steve. He did this a couple of times. Finally, as he watched Steve walk away, he said sarcastically, "Oh yeah, today must be my lucky day." Then, with his hand shaking, he put the screw in his pocket.

Steve helped the lady into his pickup and shut the passenger door. Instead of going to the other side of the pickup, he walked briskly back to Craig who was still standing there reflecting on everything that had occurred. He put his hand on Craig's shoulder and said, "That was a really difficult thing to do. You made a decision to stop that man, and I tell ya, once that happened, there was no stopping you. It seems to me, the cheetah would be in a little trouble if he tangled with you."

Craig let out a laughing sigh, reached up on his shoulder and put his hand on top of Steve's. Then in a friendly way, he made a move like he was going to put an arm bar extension on Steve. They both laughed as he stopped well short of completing the move. Craig patted Steve on the back and said, "No more stories about the animal kingdom today, okay Steve?"

Steve gave a wave of acknowledgment and Craig got in his car to head home for the weekend.

"What a week!" he said as he started his car and pulled out of the station.

෪ ෪ ෪

Hours later, when Craig would normally have been fast asleep, he lay in bed, unable to turn off the review of the week that he'd just had. From his meeting with his boss, in which he was fittingly categorized as a Caretaker, to his conversations with his fellow Caretakers, to the company meeting, and finally to the theft at the station, Craig was experiencing unfamiliar feelings that were knocking him way out of his normal comfort zone. He was absolutely uncomfortable as he began to embrace the truth about Craig the Caretaker.

He had spent the last few years passionless in his actions at his job. He didn't know how he had become such an excuse machine, but he knew that he didn't like himself very much right now. By focusing on avoiding the difficult things in life, he had made life much more difficult for himself.

Sure, the family was doing fine financially. But in this moment of honest retrospect, Craig realized he had forced the family to downsize to a point that he felt "comfortable." In his effort to avoid doing the difficult things to progress in his career, he had become a finger pointer, and therefore, wasn't taking any responsibility for his own actions. When something would go wrong in his life, it was always someone else's fault or he was being judged or treated poorly. Or it was just plain bad luck.

He recalled that last month his manager had asked him to attend a training session to improve his conversion rate. He remembered his reluctance to walk into the room and the feeling that this was a put-down. Even though his manager had explained to him that all of the sales reps with a conversion rate below a certain point were attending the session, at the time Craig wouldn't accept it.

In this moment of clarity, he recalled that during one part of the session he raised his hand and said to the trainer, "That's not how I do it!"

"I know, Craig," the trainer had said at the time, "and that's why you're in this room."

For a moment, Craig's entire body was consumed with goose bumps, as he felt embarrassed about his actions at that meeting. Instead of embracing the opportunity to improve, he had rejected any notion that he should even be participating. His best thinking had made him into Craig the Caretaker and for the first time in years, Craig was realizing this. He had been in the way of himself.

"Excuse after excuse," he thought as he reviewed his years of rationalizing. It was now three o'clock in the morning, and Craig couldn't shut it down. He reached over and gently shook his wife as he whispered, "Honey, wake up for a second."

In a fog, she said, "Craig, what is it? What time is it? Are the kids okay?"

"The kids are fine. It's three in the morning. I need to tell you something."

Expecting to hear something terrible, and therefore, becoming lucid immediately, she sat up in bed and turned on the light. "What is it?" she said with that "you just woke me up" squint.

"I want to tell you that I'm sorry, and things are going to be different from now on."

"Craig, what are you talking about, honey?" She was confused and heading for fear.

"We can be doing much better, and I want you to know that

I'm tired of just getting by. It's all my fault and things are going to change."

Craig was beginning to get emotional.

She moved closer and hugged him and said, "We're doing fine, honey. I just want you to be happy."

Craig moved her back from their embrace and looked at her, "I know you do, and that's what I'm talking about. It's not possible to be happy and half-ass it like I have been doing. I just figured that out. They call them comfort zones, but let me tell you, after a while, they're far from comfortable." Then he asked, "When would you say I was the happiest I've ever been in a job?"

Craig's wife spoke of before they had moved and of a time that Craig was attacking his sales career. She recalled that it wasn't that he was so motivated by the money, but that he seemed to love the challenge and competing with others around him, as well as himself.

"I don't know, sweetie," she said. "It just seems like you were full of, oh, what's the word? It's late."

"Passion!" he said.

"Yes. Passion," as she repeated his words. "You were after it. But you never complained that it was a grind or anything. You really were happy."

"Well, honey. That's where we're headed again. I'm sick and tired of being sick and tired. No more negative self-talk. No more excuses. I'm making some changes."

"Nice to have you back," she said as she yawned. "Can we go back to sleep now?"

He smiled and gave her another hug as he leaned over and turned out the light.

❦ ❦ ❦

After a weekend spent reflecting on his past actions in his

career and renewing his commitment to his work, Craig arrived earlier than his required eight o'clock start time. He put his briefcase down at his desk and logged on to his computer. He went and got some coffee and this time he opted to pass on making his stops at his usual Monday morning visitations. Of course, many of those people he would normally call on were not in the office yet. After all, it was seven forty-five and work didn't officially start until eight.

When he got back to his desk he reached into his briefcase, pulled out a small rolled up poster that he had purchased over the weekend, and tacked it up on the wall directly above his computer. It was a picture of a cheetah in full sprint. As he finished putting it up, he said quietly to the predator on the wall, "Too late! I'm headed for the middle of the herd."

Then he leaned to one side of his chair, reached into his pocket, and pulled out the small screw that Steve had taken out of Craig's tire. He set it down next to the phone and put his headset on. Next he pulled out his lead sheet and went to the category of "hot" leads.

"I've got a lot more hot leads than that," he thought to himself. He punched the numbers on his telephone. As the phone rang, he picked up the screw and while playing with it in his hand, said out loud, "Mondays are great days to sell!"

Chapter

SARAH THE SEARCHER

To say that she was excited about her new position in sales would be an understatement. For the past several years, friends and family had told Sarah that she should try sales and now she was elated to be part of a dynamic sales team in a growing industry.

"It will look great on your resume," her father had told her.

"You can make well into the six figures," a friend in the business had said.

"You're great with people. You should take that skill where the money is," one of her co-workers had encouraged.

"You've said you're unhappy with your company. You should go for it," her boyfriend had said.

Sarah was in human resources for a company that had just been purchased by a larger competitor. There was tremendous job uncertainty among the employees and the new parent company had a history of consolidating as many positions as possible. As long as there were a significant number of employees at her location, there would be a need for a human resources department. Yet Sarah had grown tired of all of the uncertainty and wanted to make a change.

It took a lot of courage, but Sarah finally applied for several outside sales positions in her area. She didn't know it at the time, but the company that selected her was adding several new sales reps in all of its regions. Tremendous pressure was on the management team to expand the sales force by a set target date.

Before making the leap, she had sought counsel from a friend of her dad's who had spent his career in sales and marketing at various positions. He had given her tips on how to interview and when they were through, he raised some concerns about her attempting a career in sales. "I've known you for a long time," he had said. "Sales can be a very difficult road. Granted, it can be extremely rewarding, but only the best make it look easy. Make sure you are prepared to take rejection, work long hours, seek help from others, problem solve, and deal with your income not being fixed." And there was more. He continued: "You said you were tired of the uncertainty in your current position. Well, I assure you that you will experience times of uncertainty in sales. Make sure you've thought this through."

He had emphasized the amount of rejection that successful sales people were accustomed to dealing with. "The word 'no' is something that has to turn you on, and not make you shrivel up and quit. You have to be competitive, assertive, and passionate about selling. The best sales people in the world can't imagine doing anything else for a living. Honestly, Sarah, I don't know you to be that kind of person."

The truth is that Sarah wasn't really listening. She had already made up her mind to move forward before her meeting with her dad's friend. She wasn't interested in what it took to make it, but instead was focused on her perception of sales. All that she saw were glamour, freedom, and financial reward. Heck, it even looked easy to her.

Sarah had already made her first sale. She had sold herself on a career in sales. She didn't realize at the time that the product didn't match the buyer.

The last thing that he had told her was, "I'm suggesting that you reconsider sales, but I can tell that you're going to do this. You know that you have my support, so please lean on me for help. You're going to need it. Now go out there and get some dirt on your uniform."

Sarah didn't know what that last part meant about the "dirt on your uniform," but she didn't quite understand a lot of what her dad's friend said. What she did know was that she would leave her human resources position for a career in sales at her first opportunity.

༃ ༃ ༃

She was thrilled when she got the phone call from the sales manager, offering her the position of account executive. During the call, he told her that she had a very professional appearance and was a good communicator. "That impressed the team," the sales manager had said. He went on to explain that he was tired of hiring people he called "retreads," those who had been in multiple sales positions. "I'm tired of trying to break them of their bad habits. I want somebody who is fresh and trainable. I think that is you, Sarah."

Sarah got off the phone, sky-high. She immediately called her dad, his friend, and some of her confidants. "I just can't believe it," she said to one friend. "I mean I know that I interviewed pretty well, but I had to face this committee of people and they asked me everything. Oh my God, I was so nervous, and I figured that since I didn't have any sales experience, there was no way I would get the job. But here I am! This is great!"

Sarah had joined a very large and brand-recognized national

company. The regional sales office was located in the service center, which was one of four in the nation. It was only twenty miles away from Sarah's home and had three hundred people working in it. The employees were made up of customer service, IT, human resources, and day- and nighttime telephone sales people. Additionally, there was a regional sales manager and his staff, as well as a general manager and his team who were responsible for the non-sales departments.

Two weeks of intense training followed. In her class were five other people, three who were new hires — and new to sales like Sarah. The other two were struggling sales people from within the company who were being required to take the course as a refresher. This was their last stop before termination if they couldn't make it after this retraining. The sales manager's instincts were to proceed with their termination process; however, he was under so much expansion pressure that would leave him with two more positions to fill on top of his expansion plans. Instead, and with little confidence, he opted to run them through training again.

In his heart, he knew that training wasn't their problem. He knew that they did not belong in sales, and that he and the team had made bad hiring decisions several months ago. He knew that their real intentions were not aligned with what it took to be in sales. He knew that it wasn't a fit because they were classic Searchers, a term he'd used for many years to describe those people who should never have ventured into sales. And he knew that it wasn't their fault.

The two weeks consisted of a company orientation, product knowledge, territory management, and training in selling skills. On the second Friday, with her training now behind her, Sarah returned home and was particularly excited to find that all of her office equipment had arrived. On the following Monday, an individual from the company's IT department would be at her home to set up all of the equipment that she needed to operate from her home office. On the weekend she would take all the equipment out of the boxes and have everything in place for the IT person to connect the technology. She was particularly excited when she unwrapped the small box that contained her new business cards. In print for the first time was her name along with her title of "Account Executive." Sarah was so happy to be in sales that later that evening, she proudly passed her card out to family members.

❦ ❦ ❦

The following week, Sarah was instructed to drive to an adjoining territory to meet a veteran account executive. She was to spend a week in the territory observing the day-to-day activities of an experienced and successful sales person. It was here that Sarah would get a firsthand look at what it really took to make it in sales. Sarah arrived at the Starbucks coffee shop that they were to meet at ahead of her co-worker. As she was about to walk into the coffee shop, a woman drove into a parking space across the way from her, honked and gave her a wave.

"Are you Sarah?" the lady said.

"Yes I am."

"Sorry we can't get coffee and visit, but I just got an appointment that I've been trying to get for months. I think I just wore him down. Hop in."

The account executive drove a silver BMW from the three series, in excellent condition. She moved her briefcase and some files off of the passenger seat of her car and Sarah got in and closed the door. She looked at Sarah and introduced herself. "Welcome to the company, Sarah," the sales woman said, as she extended her hand and offered a strong handshake. "I hope it is as good for you as it has been for me."

"Thank you," Sarah said. "I'm really excited about the opportunity."

As they drove to the meeting, the woman explained how she had arrived at the company three years ago. She had grown up in sales working in similar industries. For the past two years running, she'd been one of the top fifty among the company's five hundred reps nationwide.

"Number twenty-eight last year," she said proudly. "My intentions are to break into the top twenty this year."

Although Sarah was a bit intimidated, she was excited to be part of the sales team. She never dreamed she would actually be an account executive for a national company.

As they were pulling into the appointment, the woman explained that she had lost this customer to the rep she had replaced three years ago. The person she replaced had switched to the competition and taken this customer with him. "I had a lot of that at first. I lost nine major accounts immediately and they represented about forty percent of the business. I've managed to get five of them back so far, and this one would be number six. It's a challenge because my predecessor stayed in the territory and I have to compete with him. He had all the relationships. He's pretty tough," she said. "But I'm tougher," she said as she flashed a confident smile.

"Now here's what I want to do, Sarah." The account exec went on to layout a strategy that she would build some rapport, point out what differentiated her company from the competition, determine their needs, and secure a future appointment. If she made it that far, she would make a presentation at the next meeting. "Got it?" she asked Sarah.

"I think so," Sarah replied.

The account exec picked up on Sarah's hesitancy. Rather than point it out, she decided to simply provide Sarah with specific instructions and guidance. So she said, "This is what I want you to do. Just shake his hand after the introduction. Make small talk if he does, and do absolutely nothing else unless I tell you to. Okay?"

"Not a problem," Sarah said, as she felt the first sign of being uncomfortable as her adrenaline began to rise. "I'm here to learn from you."

"Sarah is here to bring me luck!" the sales woman said enthusiastically to no one in particular as they entered the building.

After a brief wait in the lobby, where the sales woman made

small talk with the receptionist, they were informed that their appointment, the buyer for the company, would see them. The meeting lasted all of about five minutes. He explained that the only reason that he had given the sales woman the appointment was because of her persistence. While he appreciated her relentless effort to secure an appointment, he was perfectly happy with his existing vendor and saw no opportunity for the sales woman and her company in the immediate future. He wanted to tell her that directly so that she would quit wasting her time and his with her lengthy voice mails in hopes of developing a business relationship.

A look of disappointment came over Sarah's face as the buyer spoke. The sales woman gave Sarah a swift kick in the ankle under the table while beaming an exaggerated smile toward the buyer. She was attempting to send a signal to Sarah, who had a look like a "deer staring into the headlights." Sarah straightened up and managed to put a smile on her face, but it didn't last very long.

Unfazed by his comments, yet in complete receipt of the message the buyer was communicating, the sales woman stood up and reached out her hand to shake the buyer's. "Thank you so much for being candid with me. I know you're very busy and I appreciate you seeing me today. Can I ask you a question before we leave?"

Sensing that she understood his position, the buyer's firm communication style softened slightly. "Certainly," he said.

"I need some guidance from you. We pride ourselves on bringing 'state of the art' product to the market for companies just like yours. My company spends more on research and development than any two competitors in our industry combined. What would you do if you were me and you wanted to keep someone like you abreast of the latest new products and developments that I don't believe, and I could be wrong, you can get anywhere else?"

Much as she tried to mask it, Sarah the Searcher was very uncomfortable that the sales woman had asked that question. In her mind, the man had just explained that there would never be an opportunity for a relationship and the sales woman was really pushing it. She mentally braced herself for an explosion.

The buyer was nodding his head as he pondered the question. The sales woman was looking directly at him with a non-threatening smile and Sarah was nervously looking at a picture to her left on the wall. She wanted out.

"You know, let's do this," the buyer said in a complying manner. "Would you send me an e-mail each quarter with any attachments that you feel may be beneficial? I'll give them a look and call you if I see anything I like."

As he handed her a card with his e-mail address on it, the sales woman thanked him for his time. With Sarah trailing a bit behind, she made her way out of the building and headed for the car.

"That didn't go very well, did it?" Sarah asked, once she had caught up.

Without slowing her pace, the sales woman said, "Sarah, listen to me. You don't know me very well, but I'm going to try to give you a lesson about sales right now. Number one: Never let them see you sweat." She pointed out Sarah's long face and her evident uncomfortable demeanor during the meeting. "You can't give them that."

"Second: Yes, it did go well. I just met a guy I've been trying to get in to see for the past two years and I reached agreement on how we would communicate. I've advanced the opportunity further than when we started the meeting."

"Oh, of course," Sarah said nervously in an attempt to avoid further embarrassment. She didn't quite know what the sales woman was talking about. In her mind, he had made it clear that there would never be a business relationship. Sarah hoped that she wouldn't run into that kind of resistance in her territory.

As they drove to the next appointment, the sales woman was fired up. "Give me another one of those because that, my new friend Sarah, was absolutely beautiful!"

Sarah was confused at her peer's upbeat mind-set. "You just got clobbered," she thought to herself.

The rest of the day and week Sarah got to see a successful field sales rep in action. They had fixed appointments with existing customers and Sarah observed the sales woman problem solve, sell deeper into existing accounts, and stay visible with many of her major accounts.

"Make sure you always have a reason when you see one of your customers. Don't waste their time," she had said. This was advice Sarah recalled having heard in her training session.

They had first-time appointments with potential new customers and they spent time cold calling in the territory in an attempt to secure meetings with "potentials" that the exec was unable to get via phone or e-mail. By Friday, Sarah had experienced a full week of sales. Meetings, cold calls, groundwork, rejection, closed deals, and lost deals. One thing was certain. To make it in this sales position, you had to have high energy and thick skin.

Without her realizing it, fear was beginning to make its home in Sarah's mind. Next week she would be on her own to begin appointment setting from the list provided by her sales manager. Sarah hoped that it would be easier than the week she had just experienced. She had certainly thought that it would be when she decided to go into sales.

"Sarah, if you need any help getting started," the sales woman had said as she was dropping her off back at her car, "make sure you give me a call. You have my cell and e-mail address, right?"

"Yes, I do, and thanks for spending the week with me."

"Remember, Sarah," the sales woman was now looking at her with her best "tough" look, "we eat what we kill." Then she chuckled, "I'm just kidding, I saw that somewhere in a movie."

Sarah gave a little laugh, but wasn't sure if the woman was serious or not as they exchanged goodbyes.

❦ ❦ ❦

On her drive home, Sarah thought about the job that she had just left. She found herself missing the security and comfort of her previous position in human resources. At that moment she had no recollection of the uncertainty that she had been bothered by there. The reality of the uncertainty that was ahead in sales was growing heavy on Sarah and she had difficulty seeing herself like the sales woman with whom she had just spent the week.

Sarah's perception of the sales life was much different than what she had just been exposed to. The sales woman seemed to thrive on things that just weren't as motivating to Sarah. A visit with an existing account, a future appointment, or any slight advancement seemed to propel the sales woman's drive to sell. All the negatives, including the rejection, the hours of prospecting with little to show for it, and what Sarah perceived as rude behavior by receptionists, assistants, and buyers had no negative effect on the sales woman. As Sarah pulled into her garage, images of antagonistic people they had encountered during the week and all of the rejection began to crowd together in Sarah's psyche. Later in the evening she would discount her fear as "new job syndrome," as she convinced herself that her own sales experience would be different.

❦ ❦ ❦

Sarah was accustomed to sleeping in on weekends, but on this particular morning she woke up well before the sun had risen. As she lay in bed uncertain of her immediate uneasiness, she began to recall the dream that had obviously brought her to this restless awakening. In her dream, she was sitting in a sold-out concert arena that must have held twenty thousand people. Seated next to her boyfriend and very close to the stage, she was waiting with anticipation to see one of her favorite recording artists. Her dream was similar to an actual concert that she had attended with her boyfriend just a few months ago.

The opening band had not come on stage yet and the usual concert activities were going on around her: people moving toward their seats, music in the background at a low volume, and the lights on as they would be prior to start of a show. The mood was electric as they waited in anticipation for the concert to begin. While sitting in her seat and people watching with her boyfriend, Sarah felt a tap on her shoulder. She recalled turning her head as a man bent down to whisper into her ear. She had no recollection of his face as he spoke.

He had one hand on her shoulder as he said, "The opening band got food poisoning from something that they ate at lunch and they won't be able to perform. You're opening tonight."

As she was explaining to the man that she doesn't know how to sing, that she's never taken a singing lesson, and that she has no intention of singing tonight, she found herself standing on stage in front of the microphone and twenty thousand people.

She stood in sheer terror as a voice on the loud speaker announced, "Ladies and Gentlemen, please welcome...," he took a breath for emphasis, "SarahHHHHHHHH!" The crowd went crazy, but then as time passed, became frighteningly silent.

Sarah recalled looking at the people as many of them stared back with puzzled looks on their faces. In the dream she had cotton mouth so badly she could hardly speak. As she looked out at the crowd, which was now beginning to make impatient rumblings of displeasure, she reached up with a trembling hand and tapped the microphone to see that it was on.

"Uh, excuse me," she said as her voice cracked, "but I don't know how to sing, and I never intended to..." and she woke up.

Sarah lay in bed reliving her dream, and thought about how rarely she recalled her dreams if, in fact, she dreamt at all. She could feel her heart pounding and could recall only a few times in her life when she had awoken in such a state. She reached for a drink of water and pushed the dream as far away as she could.

"I don't know what that was about," she said as she got up to start her weekend.

❦ ❦ ❦

While she was out during her Saturday routine later in the day, she pulled into Steve's gas station for a fill-up. It was a convenient place for her to get gas because there were so many pumps, and being a price-conscious individual, she liked Steve's prices. She also liked the small talk that Steve and she had made over the years. She admired him for having chosen to stay active versus retire and she hoped that she would be as energetic as he was when she was older.

Steve was unloading soft drinks from his pickup and putting them on a handcart when he looked up and saw Sarah. He gave her a wave, loaded another case onto the cart, and walked over to say hello. "Good morning, Sarah," Steve said in his usual spirited manner. "Should be a nice one today."

"Hi, Steve! Yes, it's a beautiful day." As she pointed to the soft drinks on his hand truck, she asked, "Why don't you get someone to do that for you?"

"Usually do. But I'm breaking in a new guy who keeps coming up with reasons not to show up. It's not a very good way to start. I get the feeling he just doesn't like what he's doing. You can come up with a lot of reasons not to get your work done if you don't like it. Besides, I need the exercise. How's that new job of yours? You sell anything yet?"

Sarah looked over at the pump as she topped her tank off. The question made her uncomfortable although she wasn't exactly sure why. "Oh, well I've been in training for the past three weeks. I really won't get started until this Monday."

She went on to explain her two weeks in the classroom, her home office setup, and her week in the field.

Steve looked over at the soft drinks and back at Sarah. "Well, good luck, Sarah. Sounds like you're pretty excited. Anyway, I have to get those drinks inside. I might have to let that boy go if he doesn't show me something. He can't do that if he's not here. I've always found that it's hard to do something well if you don't like it. I see that a lot in people, especially young people. They're searching to find themselves. That's what growing up is for, I guess. God knows, it took me long enough. A time came when I had to be honest with myself. Determine what I was good at, what I liked to do, and then set my intentions all around doing that. Anyway, I'm getting a little heavy. I'll talk to you next time, Sarah. Thanks for the business."

"You're very welcome, Steve. Have a nice weekend and I'll see you next time." As she got in her car and drove off, she said to herself, "Yeah, you've got to love what you do."

That afternoon she took a long drive through the mountains as she listened to her favorite music. She had regained the high of her new career's potential and fantasized about the financial rewards that would come from selling. She would upgrade her car as soon as her sales began to come in. She also envisioned the freedom that came from being a successful sales person. She thought about the sales reps that she had known while in her various human resources positions and she just didn't think they worked very hard. She looked forward to living the good life.

❧ ❧ ❧

Sarah the Searcher had no idea that her continued perceptions of a life in sales did not come close to reality.

❧ ❧ ❧

On Monday morning, Sarah had a conference call with her boss. Over the weekend, he had e-mailed her a list of all the existing and potential customers in her area. He had prioritized customers and provided a summary on the ones that he was educated on. As Sarah knew, the company had reduced territory sizes to add sales people in an effort to increase market share. Therefore, it wasn't as though the accounts had never been worked.

They reviewed Sarah's time in the field the previous week with the top-producing sales woman. The sales manager had already spoken with the sales woman and reluctantly recognized some early yellow flags. After describing Sarah's demeanor during the week, the sales woman had said that she didn't feel that Sarah had the "instincts for the selling game."

"Not everyone is like you," the sales manager had replied. After all, he had made the hiring decision. He had additional issues to worry about, such as more territories to fill, the three other new sales people, and the two "retreads" that he had sent through training for the second time. The sales manager knew that feedback from sales people about their peers can be ruthless, and, after all, Sarah hadn't even really started yet.

The sales manager wanted to hear directly from Sarah about her week. "What did you learn?" he asked Sarah.

"Well, this is going to be a definite challenge for me. But I think I'm up to it."

"Bad answer," he thought to himself. "Unh-huh," he said outloud. "How did the calls feel?"

"She's really a good sales person. Gets right in there and goes for it. She certainly isn't afraid to speak her mind. She's a strong personality."

He thought about the sales woman. She was definitely assertive but she wasn't nearly as aggressive as many of the others. "Uh-oh," he thought.

"Can you see yourself having similar success as hers?" He sat on the other end of the phone hoping to hear a good answer.

"Oh, most definitely! Of course, I don't know if I'll ever be as good as she is. I'm going to give sales a try, though." Sarah the Searcher had no idea of the significance of what she had just said.

Sarah listened to the silence on the other end of the line. The sales manager was mentally switching the yellow flag to red as her words "give sales a try" amplified in his head. In about five seconds, he thought of five better answers than that one.

"Could you hold for a second, Sarah?"

"Sure."

He pressed the hold button down and looked at his reflection in the window as he quietly asked, "Why couldn't she have said something like, 'I can't wait to make my first sale!' Or, 'I belong in sales.' Or, 'Nothing is going to stop me.' How about, 'All I see is opportunity.' Or my personal favorite, 'I intend to make a major impact on this territory!' Any one of those would have been great.

He took a breath, pressed back into the call and said, "Thanks for holding, Sarah." He did his best to recover from the intuitive feeling that he was having. "Let's talk about your plan for the week."

While he was careful to disguise his anxiety, the sales manager feared that he was dealing with the worst possible scenario. All indications were that Sarah was in way over her head and that he had, regrettably, hired another Searcher.

"Sounds great, I just hope I don't have the same kind of people that we were dealing with in her territory. Nicer would be better," Sarah said.

He was now unable to block out the message that his instincts were sending. Sarah's early indications of her dislikes were revealing themselves. If she was a Searcher, she did not belong in sales because:

- She perceives sales to be much easier than it really is.

- She won't do the things required to be successful because they are too painful.

- She has no intention of making the changes necessary to be successful.

- She is consumed with fear.

- She was a victim of a bad hiring decision.

- She belongs in another career because she honestly hates sales.

If Sarah wasn't going to last very long, the sales manager did not want her to go to the existing accounts that were in the territory. It never looks good when a company shows a lot of turnover.

Therefore they agreed on a plan that would have her cold calling over the telephone to set appointments with the potential "major" accounts. If she got any appointments in her territory, the sales manager instructed her to call him immediately to discuss the strategy for that account. This would also give him an indication of her success level.

He instructed her to call him at any point if ever she was stuck or had a question. He knew that all new sales people who are really working hard would have questions. They invariably get themselves in situations that they need help on. He hoped that would be the case, but his confidence level was low.

"I'll start immediately," she said. "I'm sure I'll be fine and won't need to bother you."

"Please, Sarah," he emphasized to her, "Bother me!" To himself, he thought, "She doesn't know what she's saying right now."

They concluded the call and Sarah looked at the list of accounts. The cotton mouth that she had experienced the morning after her recent nightmare had returned in full bloom. But she didn't connect the similarity between her dream and her new career. She took a sip from her bottled water and began prioritizing the calls that she would make for the day.

As her anxiety level grew, Sarah the Searcher began dialing to set appointments. After thirty minutes of calling she knew one thing: each time she got into someone's voice mail, instead of connecting to the person in real time, she was relieved. She really didn't like "pitching" to get an appointment. On the three calls that she did connect with a live body, she was rejected immediately. It made for a very painful thirty minutes.

Sarah pondered her next move and decided to try a new strategy. Even though her manager had instructed her to make calls for the day, she felt that she might be more successful driving through the territory and walking in and securing appointments. She decided that she wouldn't bother her manager with her new plan. Besides, making appointments on the telephone wasn't working for her.

She spent the rest of the morning printing directions to various accounts that she would visit. After lunch, she went out, got in her car and headed for her first target.

Sarah made four stops that day. One did not accept walk-in solicitation, as the receptionist gruffly emphasized by pointing to the sign that Sarah had missed when entering the building. It was a very unpleasant exchange for Sarah. At another stop, the receptionist buzzed the operations manager who apparently was the decision maker, and he relayed a message to Sarah through the receptionist that he wasn't interested. The best Sarah was able to do was to get the contact names out of two of the four stops she made.

In her mind, Sarah the Searcher's first official day in sales was an absolute disaster. Later that night, thoughts of the comfort of her previous career crept back into her mind. She missed the old routine.

❦ ❦ ❦

After a restless night of little sleep, Sarah got up and convinced herself that she was going to approach the day with a positive attitude. "Good things will happen today, Sarah!" she said to herself as she entered her home office for day two. On her desk was the call list that she was to use to secure appointments. Even though she had no success yesterday, she had hopes of reversing that today. She picked up the phone and decided to call the two names of the contacts that she had gotten the day before.

She connected immediately with the first call and introduced herself to the buyer. He was disinterested and seemed put off by the call. He quickly explained to Sarah that he didn't believe that her products or pricing were as good as the relationship that he currently had. Instead of viewing this as an opportunity to ask some questions, develop some rapport, and create an opening in the future to really determine his needs, she simply said, "Okay, thank you very much for your time," and hung up the phone.

Sarah the Searcher was blind. She could not see that on this particular call, it was as good as it gets. The man had actually engaged
and given her enough dialogue that someone like the sales woman
she had spent last week with would have taken advantage of.

"See, telephone appointment setting doesn't work for you!"
she said to herself. She came up with a new plan. She would write
a quick letter introducing herself to everyone on the list — well, at
least everyone for whom she had an address and contact name.
Then in the next few days she could follow up with them to see if
they had received the letter. Maybe her calling wouldn't be quite
so cold and she could secure some appointments.

She considered checking in with her boss to discuss this new
strategy and seek help, but decided that he was probably too busy
and she didn't want to bother him. The truth is, however, Sarah
was fearful that he would put her back on the phone — and she had
no intention of continuing cold calling via the phone.

She spent the rest of the morning writing a two-paragraph letter that she would send out to fifty-three prospects in her territory.
After lunch, she made labels, folded the letters, slipped in her business card, and drove to the post office to get stamps. She returned
home and finished the project, went back to the post office and
mailed the letters. "Busy day!" she thought to herself, as she pulled
back into her garage at about five-thirty in the afternoon.

❦ ❦ ❦

Sarah the Searcher was fooling herself. She hated real sales,
therefore she was going to do everything but engage in what it
took to be successful at selling. Her strategy changes and direct
mail project were just a way to avoid doing the inescapable tactics
required to be a successful sales person. It remained to be seen
just how long she would play the role of a sales imposter, but the
Searcher was beginning to look over her shoulder at the inevitable.

❦ ❦ ❦

The next day Sarah decided that since it would take a couple of days for her target accounts to receive their mail, she would input her list into her electronic time manager that was provided by the company. That way, when she did secure appointments, and things picked up, she would be prepared.

Around midday, she got a phone call from her sales manager, calling to check on her progress. "I haven't heard from you. How have the last two and a half days been?" He knew it was a bad sign that she hadn't called in two days. He had even talked to the sales woman that Sarah had ridden with in the adjoining territory to see if she had heard from Sarah. He wasn't surprised that Sarah hadn't called her either.

"I think I'm doing okay!" Sarah said, with some trepidation.

"I take it you haven't gotten any appointments, since you would have called when you secured them, as we discussed on Monday. How many calls have you made and what are the major objections that you're running into?" He could feel what was coming.

"Well, you know I made a couple of changes to that strategy early on in the week."

Another red flag went up as the sales manager listened to Sarah dance around the inevitable. "First, I wasn't having any success making outbound calls, so I decided to try face-to-face walk-ins. That was just as bad."

The sales manager wasn't shocked by her comments, yet as he sat on the other end of the phone he closed his eyes, squinted, and shook his head, not liking where this was heading. "You don't change strategy when you're new!" he thought to himself.

Sarah continued, "So yesterday I came up with an even newer strategy. I developed a direct mail letter and sent it out to fifty-three of the targets on the list and enclosed my card." She was talking fast and hoped that he didn't catch on to her nervousness. "I was planning to follow up with them tomorrow and Friday. Maybe that will work. I'm just not very good at cold calling. I don't like it very much."

The sales manager was reflecting on their interview prior to her taking the job. He was trying to pinpoint any red flags that might have told him he would be faced with this situation. They had clearly covered the amount of time that would be required to cold call. He thought about how she obviously wasn't engrossed in the sales process because if she were, she would know what her key objections or obstacles were and would seek help.

"A good sales person won't be denied!" he thought.

It was his experience that new sales people who were really working it always got stuck and needed help. He knew that since she hadn't even communicated with the sales woman that she had just spent time with in the field, the odds are she was just moving around the perimeter of actually getting involved in real selling.

"Okay, Sarah. That sounds pretty good." The sales manager did his best to not telegraph how he really felt. He had decided that Sarah was, in fact, a Searcher. Therefore, there was no point in making her do the things she found too painful to execute, even if those things were her key to success. He was now convinced that he had made a bad hiring decision and that the truth was that Sarah hated sales.

"You can't succeed at what you hate," he thought to himself. Therefore, there was only one decision left to make. He would terminate Sarah the Searcher. Continuing to hide the immediate future from Sarah, he told her that he wanted to meet with her on Friday to align their thinking for week two. They locked in on a midmorning meeting at his office.

Sarah hung the phone up a little concerned with how the call had gone. "Maybe I should have called him before I changed strategies," she thought. Then her mind moved to the big picture as she tried to envision a long-term career in sales. She was now having real trouble with that vision. "Sarah, what have you gotten yourself into?" she asked herself. Feeling dispirited and fearful from her last thought, Sarah decided to abandon the working day and take in a late afternoon movie.

"I need to get my mind off of this," she thought. She went on the Internet and chose her movie and decided she had time to run a few errands beforehand. Doing her best to distance her mind from the reality that she was in over her head, Sarah the Searcher marched out the door, got in her car, and headed down the open road. As she drove, she passed a few "target" accounts that were on her list. The sight of them was a painful reminder of her current situation. Sarah could no longer avoid feeling that she might have chosen a career that was much harder than she'd thought.

❧ ❧ ❧

Searching in her purse for some Tylenol pills to relieve her stress-induced headache, Sarah discovered that her bottle was empty. She happened to be driving by Steve's gas station and pulled into the mini-mart to relieve her pain.

She parked her car and went inside to the aisle that carried the over-the-counter medication and found what she was looking for. She then walked to the cooler and added a bottle of water. As she was paying, Steve came out of the back room carrying a large box of assorted candy bars. He proceeded to the front of the mini-mart by the cash register and began restocking the shelves near Sarah.

"How are we doing today, Sarah?" Steve asked in his usual thoughtful greeting.

"Okay, Steve. I'm headed to an afternoon movie and I need to kill the pain of this headache first."

Steve nodded his head as Sarah paid the cashier and began heading for the door. He set his box down and walked beside her. As she was exiting, he handed her a candy bar.

"Can't enjoy a movie without some candy. Try this. It might do the trick if those Tylenol pills don't work."

This put a smile on Sarah's face, which put an even bigger one on Steve's.

"Oh, thanks, Steve," she said as she put the candy bar in her purse.

"The price they charge at the movies for one of those is outrageous," he said.

He stepped in front of Sarah the Searcher and opened the door for her. Steve saw that she wasn't her usual self. She thanked him and walked out of the mini-mart and as she did, Steve stayed inside.

When she stepped out she was taken back by what she saw. She couldn't understand how she could possibly have missed those two kids when she entered the store. To her left was a girl in uniform sitting behind a card table stacked with Girl Scout cookies. The girl's vest had buttons and merit badges that Sarah assumed were for achievements and her sleeve had a patch on it that said, "Girl Scouts U.S.A."

Directly to her right and sitting across from the Girl Scout was a boy in a Little League uniform. He too was sitting behind a small table but instead of cookies, he had boxes of candy displayed. Like the Girl Scout, the Little Leaguer was in full uniform. His golden blond hair was coming out of the sides of his dark green hat with a yellow bill that had an "A's" emblem across the top. Underneath his green short sleeve uniform top he wore a yellow jersey. He had on white baseball pants and long green socks, pulled up high, old style. He even had his rubber baseball cleats on.

Both kids appeared to be about twelve years old and both were there for the same purpose. They were selling their products to raise money to support their own local organizations.

Sarah was still amazed at herself for having overlooked the two kids when she entered the store. She now stepped to the side of the doorway, paused and looked back and forth at each child. The Girl Scout was pitching her cookies to everyone who entered from her side of the building. Sarah watched this confident little girl as she fearlessly announced her intentions to every customer at the mini-mart.

"Good afternoon, would you like to buy some Girl Scout cookies? The money that we raise provides us with the financial assistance we need to keep our camp fees for all girls to a minimum. Did you know that today there are nearly four million Girl Scouts?"

The little girl was a selling machine and she had the hit rate to prove it. If someone wasn't buying cookies, she was talking to them about buying cookies.

"The Girl Scouts were founded in 1912 and all of the money that we raise stays right here in the community. And the cookies taste great too. Would you like to try one for free? My dad bought a couple of boxes so that I could use them as samplers for my customers."

Sarah watched as the girl moved the cookies from her table directly to the buyers. In turn, they gave her money, which she placed in a small metal box she kept directly in front of her. Sarah took particular notice of the girl's behavior when she would get rejected. She would thank the people and continue about her business, apparently unfazed by the declination to buy; she'd simply focus on to the next available "walk-by."

"She's really into this," Sarah thought.

The Little Leaguer wasn't having the same results, in fact, while Sarah was observing, he hadn't sold a single box of candy. Sarah could tell that the boy was miserable. He sat with his elbows on the table and both hands under his chin. He was watching the little girl work and letting potential customers walk by his table without speaking or even making eye contact. Sarah's heart went out to the boy. For the first time, she knew exactly how he felt. She decided to go over and buy a box of candy in an effort to cheer him up.

"Hi," she said to the boy who obviously didn't want to be there.

"Hi. Would you like to buy some Little League candy?"

"Sure, I'll take a box."

"You will?"

"Yes. I like candy."

He told her how much it was, handed her a box and took her

money. "Thank you," he said, as he put the money in an envelope.

"You're welcome. Let me ask you something. How come you're doing this if you're so miserable?"

The little boy looked around as if to make sure that nobody would hear him. "My mom is making me. My brothers had to do it when they played, and so do I. They were really good at it, though. I just don't like it, and I can't wait until she picks me up at five."

Meanwhile, the Girl Scout was working the people as they walked in and out of the store.

Sarah really felt for the boy. "You know, I'll take two boxes today."

"Okay," he said as he listlessly repeated his routine with the candy and the money. "My brother said this would be easy and I believed him. But I'm not gonna introduce myself to everyone who walks by like she is doing," and he pointed across the way to the Girl Scout. "I don't think they want to buy any candy anyway and I just want to play baseball. I hate this."

"Yeah, I kind of know what you mean," Sarah said, as she looked to her right and saw Steve watching through a window next to the doors of the mini-mart. He nodded his head and gave a little smile.

Sarah looked back at the boy and realized that she was seeing herself. She knew that the only sales the boy would make that day would be due to complete luck, walk-bys like herself who felt sorry for the young peddler. She knew that if he wasn't willing to do the things required to make things happen, the odds are, nothing would happen. She also knew that he had no intention of making the necessary changes to sell some candy.

"It would be too painful for him," she thought.

Nausea began to seep through the walls of Sarah the Searcher's stomach. She saw in the boy the truth about herself that she had been avoiding. She was not cut out to be in sales. The truth was that she had grossly miscalculated the difficulty level of a career in sales. Doing what it took to be successful not only scared Sarah but also if it was anything like what she had been through this past week, and it was, it would be far too painful to keep trying.

Sarah's nausea was followed by fear as she thought about her next move. The movie she was going to attend seemed like a thought from the past. She had that same jittery feeling in her stomach that she had when she woke up from her dream of the concert. Her pulse began racing and she could feel the pounding of her heart. Her breathing became very rapid as she struggled to gather herself to get out of the gas station and go make an attempt to figure life out. She was having a revelation. She was disclosing to herself that she did not want to make any more attempts to stay in sales. It was not for her.

Several seconds had passed with her just standing there and pondering her life. The boy was looking at her strangely, and asked, "Lady, are you okay?"

"What position do you play?" she said as she composed herself.

Upon being asked a baseball question, the boy took on a completely different demeanor. He brightened up and answered with all the confidence in the world. "Second base. And I made the All-Star team!"

"Well, hang in there. You'll be back on the baseball diamond before you know it." Then she responded to the boy's question by saying, "Yes, I'm fine. I have someplace I have to be."

As she got in her car to leave, she could still hear the Girl Scout pitching her cookies to a passerby who stopped to consider buying. "We have several different flavors. Have you had them before? Try one of these."

"Give it a rest, kid," she said to herself.

Her engine was running and she was about to back out of the lot when Steve appeared at her window. "Don't be late for that movie, Sarah. I always like to see the previews."

He was making small talk and she knew it. In fact, she knew

that Steve had her completely figured out. She wasn't exactly sure how, but she felt as though he staged the whole "kids selling cookies and candy" scene. She also knew that Steve was checking to make sure that she was okay.

"You know, Sarah," the old man said, as he leaned over and rested his forearms across the open window on the driver's side, "I don't claim to know too much about too many things." He paused and looked over his glasses. "But I do know this. I've known a lot of sales people over the years, both as customers and those that I've dealt with in the station. The really good ones have this in common: they absolutely love it. In fact, if you were to make a list of what it really takes to make it in sales, and a list of what most people hate to do, I bet those lists would be identical. But for these people who love sales, they sure don't hate the things it takes to be successful. Heck, 'no' turns the good ones on," as he gave a chuckle. "Know what I mean?"

Steve was waving to a customer as he handed Sarah a clean white handkerchief that he pulled from his side pocket. Sarah's eyes had welled up as he was talking and she dabbed them as she felt both relief and embarrassment at the same time.

Steve continued, "And you know, it's important to do something that you love, and I love this place, and talking to pretty girls like you."

With that he gave Sarah a wink and told her to keep the handkerchief. "You'll figure it out and you'll do just fine. Don't sweat the little things, Sarah...and everything is a little thing."

He stood up from leaning into Sarah's car and said hello to a customer who was filling up. "Easy for me to say, huh?" and they both laughed.

She thanked Steve and he did the same with, "Thanks for coming in and I'll see you next time."

Sarah understood exactly what Steve was saying. She knew he was a kind man who really cared about people. "He knows exactly who he is," she thought to herself. "That is success."

As she was pulling out of the station, she looked back and saw Steve talking to the boy and the girl. She smiled a bit ruefully and blew her nose. "I've got to get out of this," she said as she merged out into the traffic and headed home. She had opted to pass on the movie.

ǔ ǔ ǔ

Later that evening and the next day, she recalled the meeting that she had with her dad's friend prior to accepting the position. As she remembered his comments, she was struck by how true they really were. He'd said that sales could be an extremely difficult road. Although it could be very rewarding, only the best make it look easy. She could hear his words in her head: "Make sure you are prepared to take rejection, work long hours, seek help from others, problem solve, and deal with your income not being fixed."

She thought about the truth in his statements and found it curious that she had not really listened at the time. She remembered him saying, "You have to be competitive, assertive, and passionate about selling. The best sales people in the world can't imagine doing anything else for a living. Honestly, Sarah, I don't know you to be that kind of person."

"You were right about that," she thought.

On Thursday evening, Sarah decided that she would give her notice to her boss at their meeting in the morning. Of course, she had no idea that her boss had also concluded that she was not a fit for sales and had set up the meeting specifically to terminate her employment. She decided that she would return to human resources where she felt comfortable. In fact, she had a renewed appreciation for the career that she had left behind. Not to mention a new respect for sales people.

ǔ ǔ ǔ

With traffic cooperating, the next morning she arrived at the office in about twenty minutes. Even though she was early for the meeting, she had hoped to meet with her boss and get the meeting over with. On the way to his office, she passed various departments in the service center. The employees in the building now numbered over three hundred as the company's growth required adding the necessary infrastructure. Sarah walked through the customer service arena where most of the staff was. She passed by accounting, IT, and human resources.

As she was going by the HR department, she heard a familiar voice call her name. She turned to see that it was her boss from her old company.

"What are you doing here?" Sarah asked with excitement.

"Well, the company is growing so rapidly that they needed to expand the department and brought me in to manage. Apparently there was a guy who was set on getting promoted to manager. They passed on him and brought me in. After that, he gave his notice."

She leaned closer to Sarah and whispered, "You know, we worked together a long time, and while I can't go into detail, I know that selling isn't working out for you. I do have an opening and you…"

"I would love to get back into HR," Sarah blurted. "I have to tell you, everything it takes to be in sales is completely alien to my character. In fact, I'm going in to resign right now. Don't tell anyone."

"Sarah, I already know. Keep this to yourself, and I'm only telling you because we're friends. God, this is a major violation, but today he is going to terminate you."

While at first she was startled, Sarah the Searcher looked at her friend and surrendered her true feelings. "Now that you've told me, I'm not at all surprised. I probably threw off every vibe that said that this wasn't for me." She moved even closer to her friend, "I HATE selling. I would really love to work for you again. What should I do?"

"Well, Sarah," her friend whispered, "come into my office. We have a couple of minutes before your meeting."

As they sat down, the HR manager explained that the sales manager had come to her with Sarah's resume. He told her that Sarah wasn't going to work out in sales, but had noticed that they came from the same company and had worked together for quite some time. He also knew that there was an opening in HR.

"He asked me if I'd filled the position yet, and I told him that I would love to have you if you wanted to get back into it. He's going to ask you about it."

They worked it out that Sarah would meet with her as soon as she was finished with her boss. With that, Sarah the Searcher went to her meeting.

❦ ❦ ❦

Her sales manager had his game face on. Terminating people never felt good, and the day that it did, he vowed to get some counseling. He motioned for Sarah to come in and she sat down across from his desk.

They exchanged hellos and Sarah decided to spare each of them the pain of a termination. "First of all, I want to thank you for everything, but I think we both know that this isn't working out. Honestly, I'm not cut out to be in sales. I know in my heart that it is something that I just will never excel at."

The sales manager's undertaker look immediately left his face. He gave a forgiving smile, as he listened to her do what he didn't have to.

"I really like the company and the people I've met and you've been more than patient with me. If there was ever an opening in my old position of human resources, I would love to stay with the company, but I'd be kidding myself if I stayed in sales. After what I've learned about selling, I must tell you that I have no intention of going to those measures to make sales."

For a brief moment, Sarah wondered why she could not be that smooth and self-possessed when trying to sell. "That came out pretty well," she thought, as she kept her mouth shut and waited for a response.

The sales manager felt no need to disclose the termination and was relieved that a negative situation was turning positive. "Thank you for your honesty, Sarah. You know, it's hard to bat a thousand when you hire people and I think we both knew early on that this wasn't going to work. But I do have some pretty good news." He went on to explain of a potential position in the human resources department and spoke of her old boss. He told her that he had taken the liberty of passing her resume on in anticipation that it didn't work out in sales. They worked out some exit details and he arranged for her to meet with the HR manager to take it from there.

As Sarah walked over to the HR department, she felt more confident and buoyant than she had in weeks. She understood now that she'd always have to struggle just to keep her head above water in sales. It felt good to be out. The Searcher in Sarah was dead. Not because she turned things around and committed to selling. Quite the contrary, the Searcher was dead because she got out of a career she should have never gotten into.

"It's hard to be good at something you hate," Sarah said softly to herself as she walked back into her old world, "and easy to be good at something you love." And, with a newfound appreciation for HR, she stepped back into a world that she loved, feeling transformed.

Chapter

6

From the beginning of the meeting to the end, he'd brought to life "The Four Kinds of Sales People." Every person in the room now had a clear understanding and if they were honest with themselves, each had found themselves within the characters and stories he had just told. Breakthrough achievement is a personal path which is different for everyone. The leader had narrowed those differences down, however, to four different types.

As he closed the meeting, the leader addressed the group with his final comments. "And so as individuals you are at a fork in the road, and the question becomes, which road will you choose? Do you stay on your same path? Stay on perhaps the path of least resistance? Or, regardless of your current level of success, do you take the difficult road that will take you to bigger and better places in your life? One road will allow you to keep doing what you are doing, while the other will lead you to breakthrough achievement.

Only you can make the decision on the path you choose. Thank you."

There was always one moment that he found particularly special. It's that moment after the applause, and before the rush of people coming forward to talk to him. He thought of it as the "tweener" moment; it had to do with the expressions on the faces of various sales people. Some looked delighted with the validation of who they were. Some were Performers. Some were Professionals. Both types of people glowed with gratification: beyond validation, they had just gained insight on the things they need to do to move their productivity to an even higher level, and have some serenity while doing it. Other Performers and Professionals were simply grateful to have some clarity on what they should guard against.

He was always interested to see the reaction from the Caretakers in the audience. He could tell when he'd gotten to one of them. The Caretakers who recognized themselves in his stories exhibited that look of, "Uh-oh, I've been exposed." Awkward and painful though those moments were for them, he loved seeing that look, because that moment might be the beginning of the transition from being a Caretaker to being either a Performer or a Professional. It was an opening, an opportunity into a new life. Of course, there were always some Caretakers who remained in denial, unable or unwilling to self-examine with rigorous honesty. They would probably remain in their comfort zone while continuing their lackluster performance and suffering in the pain of mediocrity.

Then there were the Searchers. There would be one of two reactions from this group. On some, there would be a look of relief, surrender, peace of mind, or a release from anxiety. This was by now a familiar look to him; it said, "I'm okay after all, I'm just in the wrong career." He knew that some of these Searchers, whether beginning sales people or not, would thank him later — as would their sales managers and vice presidents. The Searchers who recognized themselves would at least look back on today as a turning point. They were the pretenders who were about to make a change, thanks to finally seeing themselves clearly.

But, unfortunately, that accounted for only some of them. The rest of the Searchers had the patented "no look." This "no look" was the same look they had worn when they walked in the room. They just didn't get it; perhaps they never would. Oblivious or in denial, they were headed for a much more uncomfortable ending than those Searchers who, like Sarah, had figured it out.

And then, the "tweener" moment was gone. It had lasted only about thirty seconds, and after almost twenty-five years of studying people, in particular sales people, he knew those first thirty seconds could be very telling.

He wasn't surprised when the first person to approach him was the same gentleman who had entered the room at the very last moment, talking on his cell phone, exchanging "high fives" as he made his way to his seat. He had pegged him as a Performer from the beginning.

"Amazing!" This character was alive and in full animation as he addressed the leader. "How did you know? You nailed me. You completely described my life! I'm a Performer. I mean I'm ALWAYS one of the top five producers. Man, how did you know?"

He looked at the sales guy and said what he always said. "I didn't know. You knew and you were honest enough with yourself to figure it out." With that, he handed the Performer a three-by-six-inch laminated plastic card. On the front of it was the company mission statement. On the back was a list of the four kinds of sales people he'd just spent the meeting discussing.

As he handed the card to the Performer, he pointed to the traits that pertained to Performers.

The Performer

- Emotional
- Intuitive
- Passionate
- Very competitive
- Extroverted
- Impatient
- Large ego
- Natural-born sales person
- Top producer

The Challenge: The highs and lows of the emotional roller coaster caused by a large ego.

The Fix: Get out of yourself and help others with no agenda other than to help.

"Do yourself a favor, man. Don't be like Parker and wait to hit bottom before you make a change. Individuals who are emotional, extroverted, impatient, and equipped with large egos can be doing damage that they don't even realize. This is especially true among top producers who are having financial success. They think to themselves, 'Why change, I'm one of the best?' Look at Parker's actions before the accident. He was pompous, self-centered, and unreasonable. Look at how he treated people. What I'm saying is that it does not have to be like that. You have an opportunity to be like Parker after his realization—helping others and getting more from his work—and without going through what he had to go through to get there. Some Performers already get it and give back to their co-workers, to the community, in order to stay balanced. Make sure you take a look at your true intentions and that you're putting your hand out to others. It really works, and by the way, you'll spend more time in the selling zone." With that, he shook the Performer's hand.

The Performer looked the leader in the eye, and with all sincerity said, "I really heard you today. Thanks."

The leader watched as the Performer walked away, looking at the box on the card that defined him. Then the Performer placed the card in his top shirt pocket. Instead of heading for the door, as he would have normally done, off to his own world of sales deadlines, he paused, looked around the room, and approached another sales person. "Maybe he's going to start giving right now," the leader thought.

A conservatively dressed, competent looking woman who appeared to take her sales career very seriously approached him after the Performer left. "I have a question, if you don't mind," the woman said as she reached out and greeted him with a firm handshake. She was confident and direct in her manner, and he could tell that she always chose her words carefully. He wasn't surprised that she had a question. In fact, he thought she probably had several questions. Professionals are analytical people.

"Is it possible, in your opinion, to be more than one kind?"

This was a question that he had heard on many occasions, particularly from Professionals, and he always handled it the same way, by returning her question with another. "How do you see yourself?" he asked.

"I'm certainly most like Paula, an even tempered, analytical, and patient individual, but I consider myself to be very intuitive also."

"Are you a top producer?" he said, knowing that this particular question would not have to be asked of a Performer. They will usually tell you in their first few sentences.

"Consistently," she replied. He got a one-word answer from a focused Professional.

The Professional

- Even tempered
- Analytical
- Logical
- Quietly competitive
- Internally passionate
- Patient
- Controlled ego
- Top producer

The Challenge: Broaden your selling strategy and extend your conservative approach.

The Fix: Take more risks in your selling game and go to the difficult places.

As he handed her a card with the "Four Kinds," he explained to her that the important thing is to understand which of the traits are most fitting to the individual. "Many of us bleed over into another, but you will always find a dominant 'Kind.' As an example, we all have a little Caretaker in us some of the time. After all, it is virtually impossible to not slip into a comfort zone at various points during our careers. I know I can be guilty of that."

He went on to give other examples of characteristics that are shared among the "Four Kinds." He said that a Performer could, in fact, become a patient individual, a characteristic found in the Professional. "The point is, in order to work on your selling game and constantly improve, you have to clearly know who you are. If you're honest about it, you have the opportunity to find something bigger, to feel better about yourself, and get better at what you do. There are emotional and financial gains to be made, if you so choose." His passion for his belief in "The Four Kinds" remained evident, no matter how often he talked about it.

With complete clarity she said, "In that case, I am a Professional, and I thank you for your time."

"In that case," the leader shot back, before she could leave, "if you want to take your selling game to the next level, you are challenged with taking more risks. The odds are your approach is very calculated and sequential. Don't get me wrong. It's all working for you, but where is the next level for you? It would be a good guess to say that you rarely extend your personality or your actions beyond your comfort level. I bet there are potential customers, like in Paula's case, that you've chosen to avoid. Work on taking some bolder actions and you'll be surprised at the results. Why wait?"

She smiled, gave a confident nod, and walked out the door.

Just then a man approached the leader. He looked like a kid who had been told to report to the principal's office. The leader knew he was about to meet a clone of Craig the Caretaker.

"I just wanted to say that today I figured out why I never hit my goals. Heck, I quit the whole goal-setting process a long time ago. Every time we're required to do it, I would just go through the motions. It never seemed to work for me. Now I know why. It was because of my resistance to change."

"What do you mean?" the leader asked, all the while knowing exactly what the Caretaker meant.

"Consciously, I would set my goals on being one of the best in my company, but you know what? Deep down, I didn't want to go through all the things you have to do to get there. I guess that's why it is called a comfort zone. I just haven't been willing to do what it takes. I'm talking about increasing my intensity while making more cold calls, improving my product knowledge, sharpening my overall skills, you know, and things like that."

The Caretaker's words were music to the leader's ears. He had gotten to one of them. "You saw a little of Craig in yourself, didn't you?"

"More than a little," the Caretaker said. "I realize now if I want to change, I have to change my thinking. I'm really tired of just getting by. Good months followed by bad ones. I really want to change that."

People like this Caretaker always brought complete definition to the leader's sense of purpose. "Look, you're either a sleeping Performer or a sleeping Professional," the leader said as he handed him a "Four Kinds" card, and pointed out the four kinds. "But right now, at this moment, you are a Caretaker putting up Caretaker numbers."

The Caretaker

- Stuck in a comfort zone

- Doesn't do the difficult things

- Hates change

- Passive-aggressive

- Inconsistent or mediocre producer

- A sleeping Performer or Professional

The Challenge: Get out of your comfort zone.

The Fix: Decide who you are, what you really want, and go after it.

The leader's demeanor turned very serious as he made the next statement. "If you're willing, and it sounds like you are, and if you are rigorously honest with yourself—and I can tell that's how you are being at this moment—then you have an opportunity to make great gains in a short period of time. Clarify your true intentions and you'll be unstoppable. I can't begin to tell you how much your sales world will change if you're willing to do the work. There is always a reason for your actions, or in your case, lack of actions. You have to define what you truly want to do. Nobody is going to do it but you. You must be rigorously honest and make a total commitment to self-examination."

Others approached and spoke with similar comments. Some had more questions and some told brief stories related to their own situations. Some came in groups and made lighthearted fun of each other with comments such as, "He's a Professional, just look at him." Or "She's such a Performer, it's ridiculous." One Performer shot back, "That's right! I'm a Performer, baby, and I got the numbers to prove it," as laughter broke out in the room.

The leader was enjoying the "seminar high" that filled the air. The "buzz" was coming from Performers, Professionals, and Caretakers who wanted to make a change to something better.

He thought about the Searchers out there and was hopeful that his words today would give them the courage to free themselves and find new careers that they truly love. He looked down at the definition of the Searchers on the card in his hand.

The Searcher

- Perceives sales to be easy
- Won't do the things required to be successful because it is too "painful"
- Has no intention of making necessary changes to be successful
- Is consumed with fear
- Usually is a victim of a bad hiring decision
- Honestly hates sales

The Challenge: Gain the courage to find another career.

The Fix: Get honest with yourself and face your fears.

He knew that it's virtually impossible to be successful in sales if you don't like it. The responsibility for success is directly on the individual, and those who are suffering the most are the ones who continue to do the same things over and over again. Yet their results are very poor. "Continuing as a Searchers is borderline insanity," he thought. "Hopefully, I got to the 'Sarahs' who were here today."

The leader made his way toward the double doors leading out of the large room. In a brief moment of reverie he thought about one more story he'd wanted to share. He could picture it in his mind's eye:

There was Steve, standing just outside the mini-mart. He reached into his uniform pocket and pulled out a small laminated card that he always kept with him. It had three simple statements on it:

- Know yourself.
- Know what you want.
- Find your personal path to breakthrough achievement.

Steve looked at the card, as he did from time to time, and thought about the *Four Kinds of Sales people*. Years and years of talking to sales people who were customers, and an equal amount of time listening to sales people who were attempting to sell him everything from auto parts to soft drinks had confirmed that it always came down to these four.

Just then, a gentleman who was obviously selling something approached him.

"Excuse me, Steve," the man said, and then went on to introduce himself and the company that he was representing. "Our best customers own stations just like yours, and we provide..."

As Steve turned his attention to the man, he was thinking to himself, "There are only four kinds. I wonder which one you are." To the salesman, he said, "Come on, young fella. Walk with me."

With that, Steve and the leader both smiled.

And then, the reverie gone, the leader turned and began walking through the hallway. More people thanked him for the meeting and he expressed his gratitude back as they exchanged pleasantries.

With a smile similar to the old man's, he said softly to no one in particular. "It always amazes me how much I learned growing up in that service station. I hope everyone is fortunate enough to have a Steve in their lives."

Chuck Mache has spent a quarter-century selling, managing, building, and leading sales organizations, with a specialty in highly competitive industries. He used his breakthrough sales approach to lead the transition of Benchmark Lending Group from a mortgage broker to a full mortgage bank, and dramatically increased the loan volume in a short period, turning the company into a mid-size player in the California market.

As Executive VP of Sales for American Home Shield, Mache grew revenues from $6M to $100M in ten years, formed strategic partnerships with other market leaders, such as Coldwell Banker and Prudential, and restructured sales teams during acquisitions.

From working in the field to leading the executive team, Mache has mentored thousands of sales professionals. Through those relationships, he discovered the four paths to breakthrough sales, and he is committed to using these concepts to build next level sales teams worldwide, through his speeches, coaching, and consulting programs.

Chuck started Chuck Mache Communications in 2006. *The Four Kinds of Sales People* is his first book. He lives in Santa Rosa, California with Cindy, his wife of twenty-five years, his three children, Shannon, Rachael, and Thomas, and his yellow lab, Charlee. Learn more about Chuck at www.ChuckMache.com.